# THE ENGLISH MYSTICS

# THE
# ENGLISH
# MYSTICS
## *An Anthology*

INTRODUCED, EDITED
AND TRANSLATED BY

## Tarjei Park

First published in Great Britain 1998
Society for Promoting Christian Knowledge
Holy Trinity Church
Marylebone Road
London NW1 4DU

*British Library Cataloguing-in-Publication Data*
A catalogue record of this book is available from the
British Library

ISBN 0-281-05110-0

Typeset by Fakenham Photosetting Ltd, Norfolk
Printed in Great Britain by Biddles Ltd,
Guildford and King's Lynn

*To Pamela, Maria and Benjamin*

God, unto whom alle hertes ben open, & unto whom alle wille spekiþ, & unto whom no priue þing is hid: I beseche þee so for to clense þe entent of myn hert wiþ þe unspekable ȝift of þi grace þat I may parfiteliche loue þee, & worþilich preise þee. Amen.

*The Cloud of Unknowing*, Prologue

# Contents

# Foreword

Why another anthology of mystical writings? The last few years
have seen such an explosion of interest in the literature of
mysticism that the market might well seem to be flooded with
translations and extracts; do we really need another one?

The answer is that we most certainly need one like this.
What Dr Park has succeeded brilliantly in doing is not only to
provide a fresh and readable version of some of the central
texts of medieval English spirituality, but to pose, quietly but
effectively, the question of whether we haven't been misread-
ing the 'mystics' rather seriously for quite a while. This
literature, he argues, is not about the assorted peculiar experiences of individuals; it is about how persons grow into the
language and common life of a Christian community, reading
its scriptures and praying its liturgical prayers, so deeply and
consistently that their very awareness of themselves is reshaped
by the great event of gift and presence that is set out in
scripture and common prayer – by the life of God lived in the
human world, Jesus Christ. Try to understand 'mysticism'
without seeing it against this background, and you will end up
with a very peculiar and distorted picture that the writers of
these works would have had a lot of difficulty recognizing.

Dr Park introduces us, with authority, to the broad historical background of the language and ideas of writers like Julian
of Norwich, Walter Hilton and the anonymous author of the
*Cloud of Unknowing*, and helps us to see more clearly what
they took for granted of Christian doctrine and worship. In his
translations he captures neatly the different styles and 'tones of
voice' that distinguish them – the deadpan humour of the
*Cloud*, the reflective slowness of Julian, gradually unwinding
the meanings of a word or a picture, the rather academic
precision of Hilton, as well as the lyrical emotion of Rolle and

the gossipy intensity of Margery Kempe. This is a relatively brief collection; but it gives more of the theological heart of these great writers than many longer books, and makes not only them but their whole world accessible to the modern reader, so that – as he says at the end of his introductory chapter – we are 'invited to inhabit the offered narrative' put before us by the authors. In these extracts, we can enter that 'life in communion' that was their passion and their sustenance.

The Rt Revd Dr Rowan Williams
Bishop of Monmouth

# Preface

Some years ago when I was an undergraduate my father gave me a small book of selected readings from *The Cloud of Unknowing* entitled *The Sharp Dart of Longing Love* edited by Robert Llewelyn who was then Chaplain of the Julian Shrine in Norwich. I was fascinated by the teachings of the book and found myself being drawn to the study of mystical traditions of theology. Here was a form of theology which was answering many of my rather twentieth-century questions about theological analogy and how far God can be said to have a personal nature. My own work on the English Mystics is part of a general rediscovery that has been growing over the course of this century. I hope that this little book of selected readings may too stimulate others.

I would like to thank the following for their personal and intellectual support in my studies: Revd Canon Donald Allchin, Revd Peter Ballard, Revd Canon Maurice Bartlett, Prof. Sarah Coakley, Dr Oliver Davies, Dr Roger Ellis, Mr Jim Garbett, Dr Vincent Gillespie, Ms Pamela Hill Park, Revd Dr Trevor Park, Revd Dr John Platt, Rt Revd Dr Rowan Williams, and Very Revd Savas Zembillas.

*Tarjei Park,*
Lancaster Priory,
Petertide 1997.

# PART 1

*Introduction*

# The English Mystics

The 'English Mystics' who form the basis of this anthology all lived in the fourteenth century. It was a century that produced a flowering of literature on the spiritual life. The most important figures in this group were Walter Hilton, the anonymous author of *The Cloud of Unknowing* and its related treatises, and Julian of Norwich. Not only did all three write against a common theological background, but significantly they wrote their major texts on the spiritual life in vernacular English.

Although Latin was still the formal literary language of the educated, Hilton, the *Cloud* author and Julian wrote in the earthy and directly accessible language that could be understood by all, what we would now call Middle English. Hilton wrote several Latin letters which still survive, yet he and the others wrote their major texts to individuals or audiences who did not necessarily have much formal theological training. The texts are therefore explanatory writings on the spiritual life, telling the reader what the life is, and how it should be lived.

The English Mystics cannot be said to form a 'school' of mysticism in the sense that their writings adhere to a common view. Indeed, in significant respects they differ in their teachings on the spiritual life. Yet this difference is primarily one of approach. They are united in their emphatic advocacy of the teachings and practices of the Church. They would not in any way see their writings as countering traditional, credal Christianity, rather they see themselves as teachers who are bringing out the latent mystical truths of that tradition. Their writings were not offered as alternative theologies, but as texts that revealed the innermost truths of the Christian tradition.

Walter Hilton was responsible for a small group of vernacular texts that were to have widespread circulation and influence. The most important of these were the two books known as *The Scale of Perfection* and the shorter texts entitled *Mixed Life* and *Of Angels' Song*. Book 1 of *The Scale* was widely copied and many manuscripts survive. Both it and Book 2, a rich and profound text written towards the end of Hilton's life, act as a foundation for understanding the *Cloud* author and Julian in that they represent a storehouse of the conventions of Christian contemplation. Hilton's writings echo with the voices of the great theologians and mystical theorists of the Christian West, Augustine of Hippo, Gregory the Great, Bernard of Clairvaux and Richard of St Victor.

The *Cloud* author similarly wrote a collection of mystical treatises. He is credited too with some highly significant (free) translations. His most famous original text is undoubtedly *The Cloud of Unknowing* which presents his fundamental teachings on the spiritual life drawn (ultimately) from the 'negative theology' of Pseudo-Dionysius the Areopagite. Yet in many respects his greatest writing is the text known as *The Book of Private Direction*, which is a later text (perhaps his last) that develops his teachings into a mysticism of being.

Julian of Norwich does not write so much about the process of mystical prayer as she does of mystical reality itself. Her text, *A Revelation of Love*, exists in both short and long versions. It is likely that the Short Text was written prior to the Long Text as an initial explanatory record of the sixteen visions she received on 8 May 1373.[1] The Long Text of *A Revelation of Love*[2] is one of the greatest theological texts written in English. It con-stitutes a journey in mystical theology that far exceeds the primary content of the sixteen visions. The visions themselves act as a textual structure around which Julian weaves rich patterns of further revelation and rumination.

There are other writers who are often included in the group identified as the English Mystics, notably Richard Rolle and Margery Kempe, and representation of these writers is made in the last section of this anthology. However, the teachings of

Hilton, the *Cloud* author and Julian are of far greater theological and contemplative maturity.

There has been a significant rediscovery of the English Mystics in recent decades, and this is particularly healthy. The English Mystics do not offer the kind of 'originality' that can be the mark of modern, transient writings on the spiritual life, but they offer an entrance into Christian mystical teaching tried and tested over centuries.

# Mysticism and contemplation

Although our writers are called the 'English Mystics', they would have less readily accepted the second term here. Instead of the word 'mystics', they would have used the word 'contemplatives'.

The words 'mystic', 'mystical' and 'mysticism' owe much of their modern meaning to later centuries. Although related words were used in Middle English, they were not used in the same way as they are generally used today. The root of these words was certainly used in the early Christian centuries, but again, in a rather more specific sense than that used today. Today 'mystical' is used to refer to what is vaguely mysterious in an esoteric sort of way. It is often used of religious practices on the fringes of the mainstream, anything from Tarot to *I Ching* to crystal healing to aromatherapy.

Such vagueness has also been a feature of much philosophical speculation on mysticism. In his monumental study *The Varieties of Religious Experience* William James identified mystical states by four fundamental qualities. They were: ineffability, a noetic quality, transiency and passivity. The first of these four, he wrote, 'entitle any state to be called mystical, in the sense in which I use the word'. James meant by 'mystical' a state of rapture and a form of consciousness lying outside our normal cognitive scope. As ineffable, mystical states 'are more like states of feeling than like states of intellect', as noetic, 'they are states of insight into depths of truth unplumbed by the discursive intellect'.[3]

Much of the subsequent debate on mysticism was similarly characterized by identifying broad categories for religious states: 'theistic, monistic and panenhenic', 'introvertive and extrovertive', the 'pure consciousness event', and so on.[4] What all of these approaches lacked was attentive analysis of what mystics actually said, and also a coherent philosophical position on the nature of language and experience. Both these attributes were abundantly present in a study made by Steven Katz that revolutionized philosophical thinking on mysticism and in so doing fundamentally undermined these general category-based systems. Katz convincingly pointed out that '*There are* NO *pure (i.e. unmediated) experiences*'.[5] Mystical experiences are always mediated by context. To say that ineffable experiences in different contexts and cultures constituted the same mystical state just did not follow; all that could be asserted was that there were various states that might be called ineffable. Quite simply Katz showed that what was 'mystical' in one religious tradition was inseparably linked to its religious context and could not be identified with the 'mystical' in a different tradition, other than by the use of the most vague and ultimately meaningless categories.

The word 'mystical' is derived from the Greek word *mystikos*, which was used about things which were hidden. Rowan Williams has written: 'The root meaning of "mystical" has to do with hiddenness, closed doors, and until the sixteenth century, Christian usage of words deriving from the Greek *muō*, "to close up" or "conceal", stayed close to this primitive sense.'[6] In its Christian usage in the early centuries of the Church, the 'mystical' referred to encountering the hidden Christ in the Scriptures and in the sacraments. It did not refer to esoteric teachings, psychological states, or exotic sensory experience, but to the person of Jesus Christ and the revealed knowledge of divine things encountered through him. In an important essay Louis Bouyer writes:

> It is very remarkable that at the moment when the language of the Christians borrows the word 'mystic' from the pagan tongue, it does not make use of it to describe either a ritual or a spiritual reality. ... Mysticism was never reduced by the Fathers to the level of a psychological experience, considered merely, or primarily, in its subjectivity. It is always the experience of an invisible objective world: the world whose coming the Scriptures reveal to us in Jesus Christ, the world into which we enter, ontologically, through the liturgy, through this same Jesus Christ ever present in the Church.[7]

The word that our fourteenth-century spiritual writers used for their form of life was 'contemplative'. The religious practice that they taught was 'contemplation'. And 'contemplation' refers to the union of the human soul with God by 'gazing upon' God with the loving perception of the mind. 'Contemplation' coheres with the 'mystical' in a Christian sense in that it refers to union with God achieved through and in the person of Jesus Christ.

In the twentieth century various names are given to supposedly advanced forms of prayer: 'mysticism', 'mystical prayer', 'silent prayer', 'meditation', 'contemplative prayer'. All these words have very specific historical meanings, yet they are often nowadays used interchangeably and indiscriminately. 'Contemplation' is the traditional Western Christian word for the forms of mysticism or spirituality taught by the English Mystics. Through a sequence of purgation, illumination and union the Christian soul becomes so purified and its spiritual senses so opened towards God in love, that it is released to 'fly towards God on spiritual wings'.[8]

# Sketches from the tradition

Although the writings of the English Mystics are intentionally self-explanatory and do not assume the reader to need much previous speculative theological knowledge, the writings themselves do convey the teachings of earlier theologians. The English Mystics would be wary of spiritual innovation, and individual originality in contemplative matters would be associated with the sin of pride. Hilton and the *Cloud* author in particular see themselves as teaching contemplative truths which have been passed on by the great Christian spiritual teachers. Four such teachers stand out in relation to our fourteenth-century writers: Augustine of Hippo, Pseudo-Dionysius the Areopagite, Bernard of Clairvaux, and Richard of St Victor.

## AUGUSTINE OF HIPPO

Augustine (354–430) was born and died in the Roman world of North Africa. Apart from some significant years in Rome and Milan, Augustine spent most of his life in what is now Algeria, where as Bishop of Hippo he became one of the greatest thinkers in Christian history.

Augustine has not always been well received in recent years, yet it must be said that much of his more negative reputation is based on fractions of his work which have been used to support later oppressive theological systems. When Augustine is read in his own context the reader is more often than not overwhelmed by the brilliance of his thought. One might well say, and not without reason, that all theology is footnotes to Augustine. His influence over the centuries was profound, and at no time was this more so than in the Middle Ages. His thought was particularly conveyed in the accessible work of Gregory the Great (*c.* 550–604) which gave the Latin West its dominant categories and metaphors for the spiritual life.

With regard to Christian spirituality perhaps the two most important works by Augustine are his *Confessions* (397–401) and his great later work *The Trinity* (399–419).

For Augustine the perception of God is through the rational soul, and is characterized by interiority and intellectual ascent (in this there is a certain Neoplatonic influence). In the *Confessions* he writes of entering into the 'innermost part' of himself where he sees with the eye of his soul an unchangeable light above himself (*Conf.* 7.10). In a later beautiful passage in Book 9, chapter 10 of the *Confessions* he describes being at the seaport of Ostia, south-east of Rome, waiting to make a voyage with his mother, Monica, when they both mentally ascend to the perception of God in a moment of understanding (*momentum intelligentiae*).

The influence of *The Trinity* upon the understanding of the psychology of contemplation can hardly be overstressed. His presentation of the powers of the soul formed the basis of what became the established teaching on the self[9] (see introduction to Walter Hilton in Part 2).

Augustine is copiously biblical and his theology is grounded in Christ, eternal Word and Wisdom of God. Furthermore, his understanding of the relationship between the soul and God is emphatically Christocentric. We reach God by Christ, that is, we reach the divinity of Christ by the humanity of Christ:

> Having become a partaker of our humanity, Christ offers us ready access to the participation of his divinity. (*The City of God*, 9.15)

> The God Christ is the home where we are going; the human Christ is the way by which we are going. We go to him, we go by him. (*Sermon* 123, 3, 3)

# PSEUDO-DIONYSIUS THE AREOPAGITE

Although probably writing in Syria in the late fifth or early sixth centuries, Pseudo-Dionysius the Areopagite, or Denys, was to have a profound, albeit selective, effect upon the medieval West. Because it was believed that he was the Athenian convert of St Paul mentioned in the Acts of the Apostles 17.34, his writings were understood to carry the secret, advanced teachings of St Paul. His writings thus had an almost apostolic authority.

Dionysius' works, *The Divine Names*, *The Mystical Theology*, *The Celestial Hierarchy*, *The Ecclesiastical Hierarchy* and his *Letters*, present three theological approaches to God: cataphatic, symbolic and apophatic. Cataphatic theology gives knowledge of God by affirmations made from creation and from Scripture. Symbolic theology is that of the liturgical worship of the Church which discloses God. Both cataphatic and symbolic theology gesture towards a divine reality beyond themselves, and they gesture towards a form of 'negative theology' in which God who is essentially unknown is reached in darkness. This is apophatic theology, which proceeds by negations. The text known as *The Mystical Theology* presents this negative theology and is translated by the *Cloud* author.

Although various individual medieval theologians incorporated Dionysius' theology, it did not particularly influence the mainstream tradition. Traditional Benedictine monasticism, for example, paid it little attention. It has been rightly said that 'Dionysian influence was important for Scholasticism, without going beyond the framework of speculative thought; it was scarcely felt at all in the field of spirituality'.[10] Yet lone spiritual writers in the Latin West did pick up on the Dionysian theology, one such being the *Cloud* author, who was primarily inspired by the twelfth and thirteenth-century translations and commentaries made by John Saracenus and Thomas Gallus.

As Dionysius' texts were translated into Latin from the Greek in a series of translations through the Middle Ages, they became augmented by aspects of the medieval theological context into which they were translated. Principally, through the influence of Bernard of Clairvaux, a general prioritizing of the affection over and against the intellect significantly altered the original Dionysian perspective. By the time the *Cloud* author is writing, intellectual approaches to God are being negated in order to affirm that God can be reached and held by love.[11]

## BERNARD OF CLAIRVAUX

Bernard of Clairvaux (1090–1153), often referred to as 'the Last of the Fathers', was the leader of the Cistercian movement for reform within monasticism. Perhaps more than any other theologian Bernard was to influence the Christian mainstream in seeing *love* as the means by which contemplative union was reached. Not only did Bernard vehemently reject secular rationalism in the human perception of God, he separated cognition and affection. Where in Augustine there was an interrelation between the soul's knowledge and love of God, Bernard contrasted the two.

Bernard's mystical theology is most powerfully presented in his treatise *On Loving God* and in his *Sermons on the Song of Songs.* He opens *On Loving God* by saying, 'So you wish me to tell you why and how God is to be loved? My answer is this: the reason for loving God is God himself and how he should be loved is to love without limit' (*On Loving God*, 1.1). In the highest degree of love the soul loses consciousness of itself, becomes nothing and is absorbed into God 'as a drop of water mixed with wine disappears as it takes on the taste and colour of the wine'. For Bernard, 'to be touched by this love is to become like God' (*ibid*. 10.27–28).

Bernard's *Sermons on the Song of Songs* is an expansive theological work on the nuptial union of the soul with Christ. In this work he presents his definitive mysticism of affection expressed in devotion to Christ. In a sequence of brilliant sermons displaying profound psychological insight he presents an understanding of the spiritual life as a moral union of action and contemplation. This union is expressed spiritually in Christ-centred love. Bernard articulates this love in a rich variety of metaphors. Christ is food, music, medicine, and the heavenly doctor.

In these sermons Bernard presents two forms of devotional focus that were to be especially influential: devotion to the Name of Jesus and devotion to Jesus' humanity (*Sermons on the Song of Songs*, 15 & 20).

Bernard's influence is noticeably present in the work of both Hilton and the *Cloud* author. It could be said that Hilton presents an Augustinian spirituality influenced by Bernard, and the *Cloud* author presents a Dionysian spirituality influenced by Bernard.

## RICHARD OF ST VICTOR

Richard of St Victor (?–1173) is one of the greatest mystical theologians of Christian history. Dante wrote that Richard was 'in contemplation more than human'.[12] Little is known of his early life. He seems to have been born in Scotland, and then in the early 1150s, probably as a young man, he came to the Abbey of St Victor in Paris. There as a gifted Augustinian canon he remained, becoming Prior in 1162 until his death in 1173. The Abbey of St Victor on the left bank of the Seine had been founded earlier in the century and rapidly gained its reputation as a place of great scholarship, particularly in the work of its leading first-generation intellect, Hugh of St Victor, who was known as 'the new Augustine'. Hugh advocated a wide-ranging form of theological study which included the arts and the sciences. As his intellectual successor, Richard directed his own work more exclusively to mystical theology and wrote two particularly important texts,

*Benjamin Minor* (*The Twelve Pariarchs*), and *Benjamin Major* (*The Mystical Ark*).

As a systematizing theologian of the mystical life Richard's influence was substantial. It has been said that *Benjamin Minor* and *Major* 'remained for long textbooks of the subject for all writers on contemplation'.[13] Both Hilton and the *Cloud* author are indebted to his work, incorporating passages from his writings. Within the group of treatises associated with the *Cloud* author there is a free translation, or abridged paraphrase, of *Benjamin Minor* entitled *The Study of Wisdom that is called Benjamin*.[14]

*Benjamin Minor* allegorizes the narrative of Genesis 29–40 concerning the twelve sons of Jacob and his wives Leah and Rachel and their maidservants Zilpah and Bilhah. Leah represents affection, Rachel represents reason, Zilpah represents sensuality and Bilhah represents imagination, that is, the four mothers represent the faculties and sub-faculties of the soul. Their sons, the Twelve Patriarchs, represent the offspring of these faculties, and the sequence of their births constitutes the spiritual sequence to contemplation: fear of God (Ruben), sorrow for sin (Simeon), hope of forgiveness (Levi), and love of the good (Judas) are born of affection (Leah); sight of sufferings to come (Dan), and sight of joys to come (Naphtali) are born of imagination (Bilhah); abstinence (Gad), and patience (Asher) are born of sensuality (Zilpah); joy in inward sweetness (Issachar), perfect hatred of sin (Zebulun), and true shame for sin (Dinah) are then born of affection (Leah); and finally discernment (Joseph) and contemplation (Benjamin) are born of reason (Rachel). Within this sequence Richard of St Victor presents a psychologically astute system of Augustinian contemplation in which God is ultimately seen in the mirror of the soul.

In *Benjamin Major* Richard presents further teaching on contemplation. He outlines six degrees of contemplation which move from imagination through reason to understanding. He calls contemplation 'the free, more penetrating gaze of the mind, suspended with wonder concerning manifestations of wisdom', it is 'a kind of sight of the soul' (*Benj. Maj.* 1.4).

Victorine spirituality was wide ranging. Beyond the educational genius of Hugh and the mystical brilliance of Richard, there was the liturgical composition of Adam of St Victor, the biblical scholarship of Andrew of St Victor, and the Dionysian exposition of Thomas Gallus. The Victorines made no false divisions between intellectual enquiry and the life of the spirit, and for this they were justly renowned.

# Religious life in the fourteenth century

The fourteenth century in England was a century of turmoil. England was involved in the particularly draining Hundred Years' War with France (1337–1453). Then in 1348–49 the Black Death swept horribly through the country killing a third of the population. There was also significant social unrest over serfdom, feudalism and poll taxes, resulting in the Peasants' Revolt of 1381 when riots broke out all over England. Those who were seen to be exploiting the poor were attacked, and this included the wealthy landowning monasteries. In London the rebels burned down John of Gaunt's palace at the Savoy, took the Tower of London and killed the Archbishop of Canterbury.

In the course of the century Church life became increasingly strained. In the first half of the century the commons and nobles of England declared their dissent over papal taxation in a series of formal protests made by Parliament. Then in the second half of the fourteenth century the Western Church itself became divided during the Great Schism of 1378 which saw rival popes established, Urban VI at Rome and Clement III at Avignon. The schism took almost forty years to be resolved (with the election of Martin V in 1417).

None of the above events in fourteenth-century history find any mention in the writings of the English Mystics. Yet this is not to say that their writings were untouched by what was happening around them. Hilton in particular refers to a world outside the direct concerns of his text. There is mention of Jews and Saracens, pagans and heretics, and it is very likely that the last category alludes to fierce contemporary debate in the English Church.

Much of this debate concerned the theological controversy generated by John Wycliff and his followers, the Lollards. Wycliff, an Oxford scholar, called into question the Church's teaching on the nature of the Eucharist, the authority of the clergy, and the restricted access to the Scriptures by their being in Latin only. Although officially condemned at Blackfriars in 1382 Wycliff inspired many poorly educated clergy, especially in rural areas, and soon after his condemnation the full Bible was published in English for the first time. The Lollards were liable for arrest from 1385 onwards, and following the statute *De haeretico comburendo* ('The Necessity of Burning Heretics') in 1401 many were burned. The use of Scriptures translated into English was then officially condemned in 1407 by Archbishop Arundel. However, the illegality of English Bibles does not seem to have completely inhibited their use, evidenced by the fact that a great many manuscripts survive.

It is against this background that the vernacular texts of the English Mystics were written. By the time Julian was writing, one had to be very careful when writing in the vernacular on matters of religion, and this could well explain the lack of scriptural quotation in English found in her text.

In different ways, therefore, the English Mystics are both conservative and progressive as vernacular writers. They are concerned to express their fidelity to the teachings of the

Church, yet at the same time they are extending that teaching in English – a language that was seen as potentially subversive by those who sought to retain power by the exclusive use of Latin.

The principal English Mystics are very much associated with the formal religious life. Hilton was an Augustinian canon, it is likely that the *Cloud* author was a Carthusian, and Julian had taken vows of enclosure as an anchoress. Having said this, both Hilton and Julian were explicitly concerned to maintain an inclusive approach to contemplation. In his epistle entitled *Mixed Life* Hilton demonstrates that the active and contemplative lives need not be completely separated. Furthermore, in Book 2 of his *Scale of Perfection* he shows a significant broadening in his understanding of contemplation, seeing it as something that is potentially open to all Christians. Julian too shifts her perspective. Her Short Text of *A Revelation of Love* is addressed to 'contemplatives', yet her later Long Text is addressed to all her fellow Christians, her 'even cristen' as she puts it.

By the second half of the fourteenth century there was a marked decline in membership of religious orders across Western Europe. Yet England still had a good variety of orders across the country. There were three main groups: monks, regular canons, and mendicant friars.

The monastic life in the Western Church took hold after St Benedict formulated his *Rule for Monks* around the year 500. By the ninth century the Rule of St Benedict was the only one followed north of the Mediterranean. Then between the tenth and twelfth centuries, as a response to a perceived disorganization and laxity in the monastic life, alternative and reformed religious orders were established. In the tenth century the Cluniacs developed a better sense of *order* by having a structured form of government. From *c.* 1050 the Augustinians developed a rather more flexible life based on the Rule of St Augustine (Augustine's *Letter* 211). Then in 1098 the Cistercians began their reform, settling in remote places and returning to earlier, more disciplined forms of life. They were followed in 1133 by the Carthusians who were given to strict personal asceticism and solitude.

The thirteenth century saw the rise of the mendicant friars, travelling men who lived off local generosity. The Franciscans (1210), following their founder St Francis, offered pastoral care and taught their listeners about the Jesus of the Gospels. The well-educated Dominicans (1218), although involved in the ruthlessly cruel Inquisition in southern France, generally travelled around preaching intelligently against heresy and leading godly lives. In the thirteenth century the Carmelites, originally hermits, also became mendicants ministering to the laity.

There was a certain amount of rivalry between the orders as to which of them led the most perfect way of life. There was further rivalry between the 'regular' religious and the 'secular' clergy. It has been pointed out that this situation was given needed Christian advice in the form of Hilton's letter *Mixed Life*.[15] The Augustinian canons, of whom Hilton was one, were popular with the laity and tended to be rather more relaxed than the other orders, compared to, say, the Franciscans, who came to be marked by internal disagreement and division into separate sub-orders.

Perhaps the most important religious order as far as contemplation was concerned was the Carthusians. In the Charterhouses of England they were responsible for copying many manuscripts on the spiritual life. As stated, it is quite possible that the *Cloud* author was one of their number. His texts were circulated by the Carthusians and anonymity of authorship was a distinctive feature of the order.

Julian was an anchoress. This meant that she had taken vows of enclosure. Entering into the anchoritic life was not uncommon practice for devout, educated urban widows. Julian herself may well have been such a person. She may well have been married and been a mother, and lost her young family in the further devastating outbreaks of plague in 1362 and 1369.[16]

It has been suggested that fourteenth-century life in England has remarkable similarity to our own with major wars, cruel diseases and poll-tax riots. However, it is possible to over-emphasize similarities and thus miss the very real differences.[17] One similarity however no doubt remains true, that for all the social and religious divisions, then as now (in all denominations), the Church was filled with faithful people who attempted to lead loving lives rooted in Christ.

# The mystical synthesis

A comparatively recent development in Western society has been a privatization of religious experience, in the sense that religious experience has been abstracted from doctrine, ethics and the community of belief. Any such abstraction is absolutely unthinkable for the English Mystics, as it is for all the great theologians and practitioners of the spiritual life.

Abstraction of religious experience from its context was already in progress at the time of the English Mystics in that it was of increasingly less concern to the theologians of the schools. Alois Haas writes:

> The fifteenth century is a clear illustration of the later, oft-lamented split between spirituality/mysticism and theology. The universities contributed to this split by fostering a progressively more abstract and methodologically structured form of theological knowledge that separated theology more and more from religious–mystical experience.[18]

Prior to this development the writings of all the major theologians of the Church were directly applicable to, if not directly concerned with, the spiritual life. One's personal spiritual life was not separable from the corporate life and teachings of the Church. In many respects the late-medieval sidelining of what we might now call 'spirituality' initiated a process the outcome of which is the modern distinction between private spirituality and public religious institutions.

This is most relevant to the teachings of the English Mystics in that they *assume* their readers to be fully involved in the corporate life of the Church. Furthermore, their specific teachings on contemplative prayer cannot be themselves abstracted from what they would have seen as the discipline of the formal daily prayer of the Church and its liturgical worship. Quite simply, the English Mystics presuppose that contemplatives will pray the daily offices and attend what Hilton calls 'the sacrament of God's body'; that is, if one wants to progress in prayer, one *must* say daily morning and evening prayer (with psalms and canticles and the systematic reading of Scripture), and one *must* go to Holy Communion. Practical application of the teachings of the English Mystics without this understanding would be seen by them as futile.

The mystical life of contemplation resides within the corporate life of the Church and is fed by its faith and order. Contemplation is a flowering of the baptismal life nurtured by the prayer and sacraments of the Church, and grounded in the love of God and of one's neighbour. Although self-evident to the English Mystics, this is something which has not always been evident to modern readers.

Disregard for context (and thus meaning) has been at the root of some twentieth-century theories of mystical states as being individual psychological experiences or states of consciousness. As pointed out earlier, such views are a categorical misunderstanding of Christian mysticism, and are quite alien to the teachings of Hilton, the *Cloud* author and Julian.

The English Mystics teach differing approaches to contemplation. Their various approaches are internally coherent, yet they cannot be assimilated to each other. This is not necessarily a problem. The different approaches are different narratives of the soul, different stories of the spiritual self. The reader is invited to inhabit the offered narrative and thereby be directed towards the climax of the narrative. These narratives of the soul function as part of the grand narrative of God which gives them context. This context-giving narrative of God is the theology held by the community of belief which gestures to the God who is essentially unknown but lovingly revealed in Christ.

Christian mysticism is thus a synthesis of personal experience with theology and morality. It is not separable from doctrine, the Christian narrative of God. It is not simply an individualistic state of consciousness. It is life in communion; more than anything else it is defined by *relatedness* to and as the Body of Christ.

## Notes

1. This is the preferred date taken from the Sloane manuscripts (British Library, Sloane MSS 2499 & 3705). The more corrupt Paris MS (Bibliothèque Nationale, MS Fonds Anglais No. 40) gives the date of Julian's visions as 13 May. For a good account of the superiority of the Sloane MSS, see Marion Glasscoe, 'Visions and Revisions: A Further Look at the Manuscripts of Julian of Norwich', *Studies in Bibliography* 42, 1989, pp. 103–20, and for a good discussion of the relationship between the Short and Long Texts, see Nicholas Watson's 'The Composition of Julian of Norwich's *Revelation of Love*', *Speculum* 68, 1993, pp. 637–83.

2. Julian's text seems to have attracted a variety of titles, most commonly *Revelations of Divine Love* and *Showings*. Julian's foremost modern editor, Marion Glasscoe, quite properly uses Julian's own singular designation, 'A Revelation of Love' (used in all MSS of the Long Text). See Glasscoe (ed.) *A Revelation of Love*, 1993, p. xii.

3. William James, *The Varieties of Religious Experience*, Longmans, Green and Co., 1902, pp. 380–1.

4. Group-characteristics offered respectively by R. C. Zaehner in *Mysticism, Sacred and Profane*, Oxford University Press, 1957, W. T. Stace

in *Mysticism and Philosophy*, Macmillan, 1960, and Robert Forman in Forman (ed.) *The Problem of Pure Consciousness*, Oxford University Press, 1990.

5. Steven T. Katz, 'Language, Epistemology, and Mysticism' in Katz (ed.) *Mysticism and Philosophical Analysis*, Sheldon Press, 1978, p. 26.
6. Rowan Williams, *Teresa of Avila*, Geoffrey Chapman, 1991, p. 143.
7. Louis Bouyer, 'Mysticism/An Essay on the History of the Word' in Woods (ed.) *Understanding Mysticism*, 1980, pp. 45, 52–3.
8. Gregory the Great, *Homilies on Ezekiel*, 2.12.
9. This particularly became the case when Augustine's terminology formed the basic psychological model put forward in the most influential of medieval theological textbooks, Peter Lombard's *Sentences*. See especially *Sentences*, 1, d, 3, c. 2.
10. Jean Leclercq, 'Influence and Noninfluence of Dionysius in the Western Middle Ages', in *Pseudo-Dionysius*, Lubheid (trans.), 1987, p. 28.
11. See Bernard McGinn, 'Love, Knowledge, and Mystical Union in Western Christianity: Twelfth to Sixteenth Centuries', *Church History* 56, 1987, pp. 7–24.
12. *Paradiso* 11.132.
13. David Knowles, *The Evolution of Medieval Thought*, 1988, pp. 132–3.
14. Although ascribed to the *Cloud* author for some time, it is unlikely that the translation is his. See Roger Ellis' fine study, 'Author(s), Compilers, Scribes and Bible texts: Did the *Cloud* Author Translate *The Twelve Patriarchs*?', in Glasscoe (ed.), *Medieval Mystical Tradition*, 1992, pp. 193–221.
15. See R. N. Swanson, *Religion and Devotion in Europe*, 1995, p. 106.
16. See Benedicta Ward's 'Julian the Solitary', *Julian Reconsidered*, 1988.
17. On this see Sheila Upjohn's typically perceptive comments in her book, *Why Julian Now?*, 1997, pp. 3–7.
18. Alois Haas, 'Schools of Late Medieval Mysticism', *Christian Spirituality*, Raitt et al., (eds) *Christian Spirituality*, 1988, Vol. 2, p. 169.

# PART 2

*Selections*

# A NOTE ON THE TRANSLATIONS[1]

In translating the selected passages I have often followed the rather more free use of words and grammar of the fourteenth-century texts. When translating Middle English into modern English there is a temptation to go for formal and precise sentence structure, yet in a significant way this limits the openness of the originals. This is particularly true when translating Julian of Norwich. In not wanting to force definitive meanings on variously suggestive sentences, and, indeed, individual words, I have sometimes retained original grammar and vocabulary. Similarly, I have sometimes retained the, to modern English, particularly *long* sentences of the writers. The temptation would be to chop them up into manageable chunks, into the kind of concise sentences modern speakers of English tend to use, yet this would significantly undermine the original flow of meaning. The original Middle English sentences can be seen as journeys in understanding. The English Mystics rarely give 'soundbites'! I hope the reader will find in the retention of occasional ambiguities greater food for thought.

# WALTER HILTON – 'KNOW YOURSELF'

Inscribed at the door of the shrine of Apollo's oracle at Delphi was the injunction, *gnōthi seauton*, 'know yourself'. And this injunction to know yourself is part of the fundamentals of Christian spirituality. Self-knowledge here is only secondarily about individual self-analysis, self-knowledge is about the recognition about what *kind* of being we humans all are.[2] And such self-knowledge is at the heart of the teachings of Walter Hilton.

Walter Hilton died on the eve of the Feast of the Annunciation just over 600 years ago, that is, on 24 March 1396. Little is known about his life, other than that he seems to have taken his degree at Cambridge University (in Canon Law), that he became for a while a hermit, and then an Augustinian canon of Thurgarton Priory in Nottinghamshire. Of the English Mystics Hilton is the formal theologian. His writings show him to be thoughtful, comprehensive and systematic, and behind his writings, if we dare make such a leap, we sense a kindly and learned man. His most important works are the two books known as Book 1 and Book 2 of *The Scale of Perfection*, that is, the Ladder of Perfection. This title is not Hilton's own, but a later title devised possibly by a monastic copyist. One early MS carries the title, *The Reforming of Man's Soul*, and this is more in tune with Hilton's own language of the human soul being reformed so that the image of God clearly reflects God. *The Scale of Perfection* was written in response to a request to Hilton by a devout woman who desired teaching on the life of contemplation. Consequently, *The Scale* is not a dry and bookish book, but is an accessible and readable account of what contemplation means.

For Hilton contemplation is both the process leading to and the state of union with God. Contemplation means withdrawing the mind from the confusions and chaos of the outside world and looking with 'the spiritual eye' within the human soul to find God. If the rational aspect of the human soul is created in the image of God, then in directing the mind's gaze towards the human soul God will be seen. As Hilton writes: 'For your soul is a mirror in which you shall see God spiritually' (*Scale 2*, ch. 30). Again, the basic idea is 'know yourself'.

This teaching on self-knowledge is ultimately derived from Augustine, and it is a basic axiom of Christian spirituality. As Augustine writes: 'By knowing myself I shall know you',[3] and again in the Pseudo-Augustinian text *On the Spirit and the Soul*: 'And so by knowing ourselves we come to the knowledge of God.'[4] Furthermore, the idea that the rational soul is a mirror that reflects God is similarly derived from Augustine. In his great book *The Trinity* he writes: 'So what we have been trying to do is somehow to see him by whom we were made by means of this image which we ourselves are, as through a mirror' (*Trin.* 15.8.14). This Augustinian tradition surfaces in the great medieval flowering of Augustinian spirituality that was the Abbey of St Victor in Paris. As the great mystical theologian Richard of St Victor writes: 'The rational soul discovers without doubt that it is the foremost and principal mirror for seeing God. ... Whoever thirsts to see his God – let him wipe his mirror, let him cleanse his spirit' (*Benjamin Minor*, ch. 72). The rational human soul created in the image of God functions then as a mirror in which God is reflected. Thus, in effect Hilton tells his readers, 'Don't think that God is just somewhere "out there", God is as close as your own soul, seek God within yourself. If you wish to know God, know yourself'.

From the Fathers of the Church onwards, orthodox, catholic Christianity has taught that the image of God resides in the soul. We do not reflect God in our creaturely physicality, God is not a physical creature; we reflect God in what we might metaphorically call the 'inner' self, the self conceived spiritually, the soul. And if the image of God reflects God, then God *as Trinity* must be reflected in the soul. The soul is not a monolithic entity, but contains a living trinitarian mirror of the divine Trinity. In knowing ourselves we come to know ourselves as being created in the image of God, which is a created trinity that reflects the uncreated Trinity.

Much of this is derived from Augustine's great work *The Trinity* as mediated by the Augustinian tradition, especially by that as found at the Abbey of St Victor. The stripped down theory of the soul here is that the soul contains a trinity of memory, understanding and will. These three terms represent the Augustinian terms: *memoria*, *intelligentia*, and *voluntas*. The first of these terms, *memoria*, is much more than memory or even consciousness, it is an aspect of the whole mind, conscious and unconscious. Similarly, *intelligentia* means rather more than its derivative, intelligence, meaning something like understanding. And *voluntas* is explicitly associated with love, as Augustine puts it: '. . . the will, or the love which is will in fuller strength' (*Trin*. 15.21.41).

By the Middle Ages Augustine's system, which was most subtly integrated, had become a more rigid faculty-based psychology, to the point that by the time Walter Hilton recasts it, he writes of the one soul that has three distinct powers: 'mynde, reson and will'. Hilton's psychological model is the traditional Augustinian model of the Christian West. In essence it is: The human soul contains a created trinity of mind, reason and will (*memoria, intelligentia et voluntas*) that reflects the uncreated divine Trinity's normative modes of disclosure of power, wisdom and goodness (*Potentia, Sapientia et Bonitas*).[5] That is, the soul's mind, reason and will reflect the power of the Father, the wisdom of the Son and the goodness of the Holy Spirit. We might represent it diagrammatically in this way:

| THE SOUL | GOD | |
|---|---|---|
| Mind (*memoria*) | Power (*Potentia*) | Father |
| Reason (*intelligentia*) | Wisdom (*Sapientia*) | Son |
| Will (*voluntas*) | Goodness (*Bonitas*) | Holy Spirit |

Hilton does not speculate much upon mind as a power of the soul; it acts as a foundation to the soul, with reason and will as active powers. The Middle English word 'mynde' can mean both memory (*memoria*) and mind (*mens*) and both these meanings are present in the way Hilton uses the word. Mind functions as the 'storehouse' with reason and will as the active powers in the contemplative process.

Now all this theory might seem rather removed from a vibrant spirituality. Yet it is the basis of much popular psychology, even the kind often preached from pulpits. It is not uncommon to hear distinctions being made between the head and the heart, what we know and what we feel. And it is a similar dual system of reason and will, of knowledge and love, that governs Hilton's teaching on contemplation.

The structure of contemplative prayer is that by knowledge we develop a loving desire for God. The powers of reason and will are the powers for the knowledge and love, the cognition and volition, that bring about contemplative union with God. This union with God is, for Hilton, the perception of God in the human soul.

Much of all this might sound rather dry. What perhaps stops it being so is that all this theory is manifest in the person of Jesus Christ encountered within. It is Jesus who calls the contemplative deep within the soul and it is Jesus who is encountered by the contemplative: 'Delve deep in your heart, for therein is Jesus hidden. ... The lantern of your soul is reason, by which the soul can see all spiritual things. By this lantern you can find Jesus' (*Scale 1*, chs 47, 48). For Hilton the rational soul is not just the theoretical image of God, but is the actual image of Jesus. When the contemplative prays in faith with true love, the spiritual eye of the soul, reason, sees Jesus reflected in the pure soul, and in Jesus the contemplative encounters the divine Trinity itself indwelling in the divinity of Jesus.

*

## Physical activity and spiritual activity

Dear friend in Christ, there are two types of state in Holy Church by which Christian souls please God and get to the bliss of heaven. The one is physical, and the other is spiritual.

Physical activity is principally for worldly men or women who have lawful, worldly goods and who are willingly involved in worldly business. It is also for all young people who are starting out and have newly arrived out of worldly sin to the service of God, so that they can break down the disobedience of the body by reason and by such physical activity so that it becomes supple and ready, and not resistant to the spirit in spiritual activity – because the physical was made for the spiritual, and not the spiritual for the physical. Physical activity goes before, and the spiritual comes after. As St Paul says, *Non quod prius spirituale, sed quod prius animale, deinde spirituale*,[6] 'Spiritual work does not come first. Physical work done by the body comes first, and then comes spiritual work.'

By physical work you should understand all sorts of good activities that your soul does by its senses and that your body also does, those relating to yourself, such as fasting, keeping vigil and controlling physical desire by other penances, those relating to fellow Christians, such as your fulfilling the physical and spiritual deeds of mercy, and those relating to God, such as suffering all kinds of physical hardship for the love of righteousness. All these activities done in faith please God, but without faith they are nothing. Whoever wants to be occupied spiritually, it is effective and profitable for them if they are tested well and for a long time in physical activity, because these physical activities are a token and a revelation of moral virtues, without which a soul is not able to work spiritually.

What are all your activities worth, whether physical or spiritual, unless they are done righteously and reasonably for God? In truth, absolutely nothing. But do not leave the activities to which you are bound by charity, rightness, and reason for another activity to which you are not really bound – as it were for the greater pleasure of God, because that is not correct worship of God. It would be as though you were honouring Christ's head and face and adorning it beautifully and elaborately, but leaving the rest of his body ragged and torn. By doing this you would not be honouring him. It would be an insult (and no honour) to a person to array their head with jewels and precious stones, and to leave their body as naked and bare as a beggar. So it is spiritually; it is no honour to God to crown Christ's head and leave his body bare.

You should understand that our Lord Jesus Christ is the head of the spiritual body which is Holy Church. The parts of this body are Christian people everywhere. Some people are arms, some are feet, and some are other parts, depending on what they do in their lives. If you are busy with all your strength in decorating his head – that is, by honouring him in meditation and devotion by recollecting his Passion or his life – and you forget his feet, which are all your fellow Christians, you are not pleasing him. You are not honouring him. You are kissing his mouth in devotion and spiritual prayer, while at the same time you are treading on his feet and defiling them in so far as you will not tend to them. For, truly, he will thank you more for washing his feet, than for all the precious adornment of his head that you might make in meditation on him.

From *Mixed Life*

# *The active life and the contemplative life*

The active life lies in love and charity shown outwardly by good, physical works, in fulfilling God's commandments and in the seven deeds of mercy, both physical and spiritual, towards our fellow Christians.[7] The active life is for all worldly people who have riches and plenty of worldly goods. It is also for all others who have state, office or cure over other people, and have wealth to spend (whether they are educated or not, whether they are religious or not). It is generally for all worldly people. In the works of the active life, both physical and spiritual, worldly people are all bound to act by their power and knowledge as reason and discernment demand. If one has a lot, then help a lot. If one has a little, then help a little. And if one has nothing, then be of good will.

Yet a further part of the active life lies in great physical activities which a person must do (such as fasting, keeping vigil, and other severe forms of penance) in order to reproach their physical bodies with discernment for sins that have been committed, and by such penance control lusts and desires of the body in order to make it obedient and open to the will of the spirit. These works, although they are active, help greatly and, if used with discernment, can initially direct a person towards contemplation.

The contemplative life lies in perfect love and charity experienced inwardly by spiritual virtues and by the true knowledge and sight of God and of spiritual realities. The contemplative life is for those who, for the love of God, leave all worldly riches, honours and outward business, and to the full extent of their power and ability give themselves, both body and soul, to the service of God by spiritual occupation.

The contemplative life has three parts. The first part is the knowledge of God and spiritual realities acquired by reason, by human teaching and by the study of Holy Scripture. This knowledge is without the spiritual affection or inner savour which is experienced by the special gift of the Holy Spirit. This first part is particularly experienced by some educated people and great scholars, who by long study of Holy Scripture come to this knowledge, more or less depending on the natural intelligence and perseverance in study which is the gift God gives to everyone who uses their reason. This knowledge is good, and it may be called a part of contemplation in as much as it is a sight of truth and a knowledge of spiritual realities. Nevertheless, it is but a figure and a shadow of true contemplation, because it does not have the spiritual savour of God or the inner sweetness of love, which cannot be experienced unless the person loves greatly, because that is the Lord's fount to which no stranger may come.

The second part of contemplation lies principally in affection, without the light of the understanding of spiritual realities. This part is more typical of simple and uneducated people who give themselves wholly to religious devotion. It is experienced in this way: a man or woman in meditation of God can feel a fervour of love and spiritual sweetness by the recollection of Christ's Passion or of any of his human actions; or they can feel a great trust in the goodness and mercy of God because of the forgiveness of sins, and God's great gifts of grace. They might feel dread in their affection with great reverence for the secret judgements of God which they cannot see, or for God's righteousness; or in prayer they might feel the thought of their heart rise up from all earthly things, rising with all its powers into God by fervent desire and with spiritual delight. During all this they have no clear sight in the understanding of spiritual realities, or of the secret mysteries of Holy Scripture in particular, but at this time they do think that nothing pleases them so much as to pray or think as they do for the savour, delight and comfort that they find. And yet, they cannot explain well what is happening, but they *feel* it well.

The third part of contemplation, which is as perfect as it can be here, lies in both cognition and affection, that is to say, in knowing and perfect loving of God. And that is when the soul is first cleansed from all sin and reformed by fullness of virtues to the image of Jesus. It is then visited and taken up from all earthly and fleshly affections, from vain thoughts and imaginations of all physical reality, and you are, so to speak, powerfully ravished out of the physical senses, and then enlightened by the grace of the Holy Spirit so by understanding you can see Truth (which is God) and also spiritual things, with a soft, sweet, burning love for God – so perfectly that by the ravishing of this love the soul is for a time united and conformed to the image of the Trinity. The beginning of this contemplation may be experienced in this life, but the fullness of it is kept in the bliss of heaven. Of this uniting and conforming St Paul speaks thus, *Qui adheret Deo, unus spiritus est cum illo*,[8] that is to say, 'Whoever by ravishing of love is fastened to God, then God and the soul are not two, but one, not in flesh but in one spirit.' Truly, in this union is the marriage made between God and the soul which shall never be broken.

*Scale 1*, chs 2, 3, 4, 5, 8

# The physical senses

By what I have said you might somewhat understand that visions or revelations of any sort of spirit (whether appearing physically or in the imagination, asleep or awake), or else any other experience in the physical senses that seems spiritual, such as hearing, taste, or fragrance, or any experienced heat that seems like a glowing and warming fire in the chest or in any other part of the body, or anything that may be experienced by physical sense, however comfortable or pleasing it is – all of these are not truly contemplation. They are simple and secondary.

If it is the case that you see any sort of light or brightness with the physical eye or in the imagination beyond what everybody can see, or if you hear any wonderful sound with your physical ears, or have any sudden savour in your mouth other than what is natural, or any heat in your chest as if it were fire, or any sort of delight in any part of the body; or if a spirit physically appears to you (such as an angel) to comfort you and teach you, or if you have any such experience which you well know does not come from yourself or any other physical creature, be wary at that time (or soon after) and wisely watch the stirring of your heart. If you are stirred because of the pleasure you feel to withdraw your heart from spiritual activity (from your prayers and from thinking about yourself and your faults, from the inward desire of virtues and spiritual knowledge and experience of God) in order to set your heart, your affection, your delight, and your rest principally in this physical experience, supposing that it comprises heavenly joy and the bliss of angels, and you therefore think that you should neither pray nor think of anything else, but attend to this alone in order to maintain it and delight in it, then this physical experience is suspect and derives from the enemy, the devil. Therefore, however pleasant and wonderful it is, refuse it and do not assent to it. Because this is the trick of the enemy: when he sees a soul devoting itself to spiritual activity he is especially angry, because there is nothing that he hates more than seeing a soul in a sinful body truly experiencing the savour of the spiritual knowledge and love of God. If the devil cannot hinder a soul by open bodily sin, he will hinder it with the vanity of physical savours or sweet sensations in order to bring a soul into spiritual pride and a false sense of security where it supposes that it has had an experience of heavenly joy and that it is half in paradise with all the delight that it experiences, when in reality it is near the gates of hell. So by pride and presumption the soul can fall into errors or fantasies, or into other physical and spiritual dangers.

*Scale 1*, chs 10, 11

# *Where to direct your thought in prayer*

In your prayer you must not set your heart to any physical thing, but all your work must be to withdraw your thought from all perception of all physical things, so that your desire might be, as it were, bare and naked of all earthly things, and forever rising upwards into God, whom you may neither physically see, nor imagine in a physical likeness. But you may experience God's goodness and grace when your desire is eased, helped and, as it were, made free from all fleshly thoughts and affections, when it is greatly lifted up by a spiritual power into the spiritual savour and delight of God and held therein for much of the time of your prayer so that you have no great consciousness of any earthly thing, or at least are barely harmed by it. If you pray like this, then you pray well, because prayer is nothing else but a desire of the heart rising into God by a withdrawal from all earthly thoughts. So prayer is likened to a fire which, by its nature, leaves the depth of the earth and always rises up into the air. In the same way desire in prayer, when it is touched and set alight by the spiritual fire which is God, is always naturally rising to God from whom it came.

*Scale 1*, ch. 25

# The fire of love

Everyone who speaks of the fire of love does not know well what it is, because what it is I cannot tell you, apart from this, that it is neither physical, nor is it physically experienced. A soul may experience it in prayer or in devotion, a soul which is in the body, but it does not experience it by the physical senses. Although the fire of love if present in a soul may create a sense of heat in the body, as if it were warmed by a pleasing work of the spirit, nevertheless, the fire of love is not physical, because it is only in the spiritual desire of the soul. This is of no doubt to a man or woman who experiences and knows devotion, but some people are simple, and suppose because it is called fire that it should be hot as physical fire is, and for this reason I have said what I have said.

*Scale 1*, ch. 26

# Three kinds of prayer

You should understand that there are three kinds of prayer. The first is the prayer of speech created specially by God (as is the Lord's Prayer), that made more generally by the ordinances of

Holy Church (such as Mattins, Evensong and the Hours), and also that made by devout people from other special sayings.

This kind of prayer is the most helpful spiritual occupation for every person at the beginning of their spiritual life. Because a person is initially rude, boisterous and fleshly (unless they have more grace) they cannot think spiritual thoughts in meditation, as their soul is not yet cleansed from old sin. Therefore, I think it is most helpful if they use this kind of prayer, that is, the Lord's Prayer, the Hail Mary, and the Psalter. A person cannot run easily by spiritual prayer when their feet of knowledge and love are sick with sin, they need to have a secure staff on which to hold. This staff is the special prayer of speech, ordained by God and Holy Church for the help of the soul, by which the soul of a fleshly person which is always falling downwards into worldly thoughts and fleshly affections will be lifted up from them and held as by a staff. The soul will be fed with the sweet words of the prayer as a child is with milk, and governed by it so that it does not fall into errors or fantasies by its own vain meditation, because in this type of prayer there is no deceit for those who will steadfastly and meekly work within it.

Some people at the beginning of their spiritual life or soon after, when they have experienced a little bit of spiritual comfort (either in devotion or in knowledge) and are not yet fully stable, leave such vocal prayer too soon, and occupy themselves wholly with meditation. They are not wise. In their meditation they imagine and think of spiritual things by their own senses and follow their physical sensations. They have not yet received the appropriate grace and therefore often, through lack of discernment, overwork their senses and damage themselves. In this way they fall into fantasies and deceptions or into open errors, and by such vanities hinder the grace that God gives them. The cause of all this is a secret pride and presumption. When they have experienced a little grace they believe it to be so great, surpassing others, that they fall into vainglory, and in so doing lose the grace they have received.

The second kind of prayer is by speech, but it is not with fixed, particular words. It is when a man or a woman feels the grace of devotion by the gift of God, and in their devotion speak to God as if they were physically in God's presence, with such words as best fit how they are stirred at the time and which come to their mind following the various rewards which they feel in their heart.

The third kind of prayer is only in the heart, without speech, with a great tranquillity of body and soul. It is necessary for those who want to pray well in this way to have a clean heart, because it belongs to such men and women who by sustained physical and spiritual work (or else by the sharp strikings of love which I have mentioned) come into rest of spirit. In this way, their affection is turned into spiritual savour, and so they pray continually in their heart, and glorify and praise God without great hindrance by temptations or vanities. Of this kind of prayer, St Paul says, *Nam si orem lingua, spiritus meus orat, mens autem sine fructu est. Quid ergo? Orabo spiritu, orabo et mente; psallam spiritu, psallam et mente.*[9] This is as much as to say, 'If I pray with my tongue only, by the will of the spirit and by work, the prayer is rewarding, but my soul is not fed, because it does not experience the fruit of spiritual sweetness by understanding.' 'What shall I do then?' says St Paul, and he answers and says, 'I shall pray by the work and desire of the spirit, and I shall pray also more inwardly in my spirit without work by the experience of spiritual savour and the sweetness of the love and the sight of God, by which sight and experience of love my soul shall be fed.' Thus, as I understand it, St Paul prayed. In Holy Scripture our Lord speaks figuratively of this kind of prayer in this way: *Ignis in altari meo semper ardebit, et cotidie sacerdos surgens mane subiciet ligna ut ignis non extinguatur.*[10] This is as much as to say, 'The fire of love shall always be lit in the soul of a devout and clean man or woman (which is the altar of our Lord), and the priest shall each day at morning lay sticks and nourish the fire.' That is to say, 'A person shall by holy psalms, clean thoughts, and fervent desires nourish the fire of love in their heart, so that it never goes out.' This rest our Lord gives to some of his servants as a reward for their work, and as a shadow of the love which they shall have in the bliss of heaven.

*Scale 1*, chs 27, 28, 29, 32

# The opening of the spiritual eye

When the recollection of Christ's Passion or any aspect of his humanity is made in your heart by a spiritual sight, and when accompanied by a devout affection, know well that this is not of your own working, nor is it the pretence of a wicked spirit, but it is by the grace of the Holy Spirit. For it is an opening of the spiritual eye into Christ's humanity, and it may be called the fleshly love of God (as St Bernard calls it),[11] inasmuch as it is set in the fleshly nature of Christ. It is truly good and a great help in destroying great sins, and a good way to come to virtue, and after that come to contemplation of Christ's divinity. For a person will not commonly come to spiritual delight in contemplation of Christ's divinity unless they first come by the bitter and compassionate imagination of his humanity. This is what St Paul did, as first he said this: *Nihil indicavi me scire inter vos nisi Iesum Christum et hunc crucifixum,*[12] 'I showed you absolutely nothing of what I knew, except Jesus Christ and him crucified,' as if he had said, 'My knowledge and my faith is in the Passion of Christ alone.' He therefore also said, *Mihi autem absit gloriari nisi in cruce Domini nostri Iesu Christi,*[13] 'Forbid me any kind of joy and pleasure, except in the cross and in the Passion of our Lord Jesus Christ'; and so he said thus: *Predicamus vobis Christum Dei virtutem, et Dei sapientiam*,[14] 'First I preached to you of the humanity and the Passion of Christ, now I preach to you of the divinity and power of Christ, and the endless wisdom of God.'

*Scale 1*, ch. 35

# The powers of the soul: mind, reason and will, the image of the Trinity

The human soul is a life made up of three powers – mind, reason, and will – which are in the image and likeness of the blessed Trinity, whole, perfect, and righteous. The mind was made mighty and steadfast by the Father Almighty so that it might hold him without forgetting, distraction, or hindrance from any creature, and so it has the likeness of the Father. The reason was made clear and bright without any error or darkness (as far as a soul can be in this unglorified body), and so it has the likeness of the Son, who is endless Wisdom. And the loving will was made clean, burning towards God without the carnal love of the flesh or of any creatures, by the supreme goodness, and so it has the likeness of the Holy Spirit, which is blessed Love. So the human soul, which may be called a created trinity, was filled with the mind, sight, and love of the uncreated, blessed Trinity.

*Scale 1*, ch. 43

# Reforming the image of the Trinity

We are restored again in hope by the Passion of our Lord to the dignity and the bliss which we had lost by Adam's sin; and although we might never get it here fully, we should, however, desire that we may receive here in this life a figure and a likeness of that dignity, that our soul might be reformed (as it were in a shadow) by grace to the image of the Trinity which we had by nature, and afterwards shall have fully in bliss; because that is the life which is truly contemplative (beginning here in that experience of love and spiritual knowledge of God, by opening of the spiritual eye) and which shall never be lost or be taken away, but the same shall be fulfilled in another way in the bliss of heaven. Our Lord promised this to Mary Magdalen, who was a contemplative, and therefore said of her, *Maria optimam partem elegit, quae non auferetur ab ea,*[15] that Mary had chosen the best part (that is, the love of God in contemplation) for it shall never be taken away from her. I am not saying that you can recover in this life as whole or as perfect a purity, innocence, knowledge and love of God as you had before the Fall, nor as you shall have in heaven; nor may you escape all the wretchedness and the pains of sin, nor can you in this life of mortal flesh fully destroy and quench the false love of self within you, nor flee from normal sins (because unless stopped by a great fervour of love such sins will always spring out of your heart as waters run from a stinking well). If you cannot quench it, I would hope that you might somewhat abate it and come to that purity as close as you can, because our Lord promised the children of Israel when he led them into the Promised Land, and through them symbolically all Christians, *Omne quod calcauerit pes tuus, tuum erit.*[16] That is to say, 'As much land as you can tread on here with your foot of true desire, as much shall you have in the Promised Land, that is, in the bliss of heaven when you get there.'

*Scale 1*, ch. 45

# How and where Jesus may be found

If you want to find Christ, light up a lantern, which is God's word. As David says, *Lucerna pedibus meis verbum tuum*,[17] 'Lord, your word is a lantern to my feet.' By this lantern you shall see where he is, and how you shall find him, and if you will, you can with this light up another lantern, that is, the reason of your soul, for as our Lord says, *Lucerna corporis tui est oculus tuus*,[18] 'The lantern of your body is your physical eye.' In the same way it may be said that the lantern of your soul is reason, by which the soul can see all spiritual things. By this lantern you can find Jesus.

If you had lost all the reason of your soul by the Fall, your soul would never have found Christ again. But he left you your reason, and so he is in your soul, and will never be lost from it.

*Scale 1*, chs 48, 49

# The likeness of Christ

St Paul speaks of being conformed to the likeness of Christ in this way: *Filioli, quos iterum parturio, donec Christus formetur in vobis*,[19] 'My dear children, whom I bear as a woman bears a child until Christ is again formed in you.' You have conceived Christ by faith, and he has life in you inasmuch as you have a good will and a desire to serve him and please him, but he is not yet fully formed in you, nor you in him by the fullness of love. Therefore St Paul bore you and me and others in travail, as a woman bears a child, until the time that Christ has his full form in us and we in him. Whoever hopes to come to the practice and full use of contemplation, and does not come by this way (that is to say, who does not come by the fullness of virtue), does not come by the door, and therefore will be thrown out as a thief. I am saying nothing other than that a person may, by the gift of God, have on occasions a taste and a glimmering of the contemplative life, some people at the beginning, but they will not have the solid experience of it, because Christ is the door and the doorkeeper, and without his leave and his mark no one can come in. As he himself says, *Nemo venit ad Patrem nisi per me*,[20] 'No one comes to the Father but by me'; that is to say, no one may come to the contemplation of the godhead unless they are first reformed by the fullness of humility and charity to the likeness of Jesus in his humanity.

*Scale 1*, ch. 91

# *Hearing the song of angels*

Our Lord also comforts a soul by angels' song. What that song is may not be described by physical comparison, because it is spiritual, and beyond any kind of imagination or reason. It may be experienced and perceived in a soul, but it cannot be explained. Nevertheless, I shall tell you what I think about it.

When a soul is purified by the love of God, illuminated by wisdom, and made steady by the power of God, the eye of the soul is opened to perceive spiritual things, and virtues, angels, holy souls and heavenly things. Then the soul is able, because of its purity, to experience the touching and speaking of good angels. This touching and speaking is spiritual and not physical, because when the soul is lifted and ravished out of physical sensuality and consciousness of any earthly things it enters the great fervour of the love and light of God. If our Lord then grants it, the soul may hear and experience heavenly sound, made by the presence of angels in loving God. Not that this song of angels is the supreme joy of the soul; but because of the difference in purity between the human soul in the flesh and an angel, a soul may not hear it except by being ravished in love, and for this it needs to be completely purified, and filled with much love, if it is to hear heavenly sound.

Nevertheless, some people are deceived by their own imagination or by the illusion of the enemy, the devil, in this matter. Some people when they have worked hard both physically and spiritually in destroying sins and gaining virtues, and perhaps have received by grace a certain amount of rest and a clear conscience, immediately leave their prayers, their reading of Scripture, their meditations on the Passion of Christ, and the consciousness of their wretchedness; then, before they have been called by God, they gather their senses together to seek and to behold heavenly things by violence, or, before their eye is made spiritual by grace, they overwork their senses by imagination, and by undiscerning work they turn their brain inside their head, shattering the powers and senses of the soul and of the body; and then, out of feebleness of the brain, they think that they hear wonderful sounds and songs; and all of this is nothing but a fantasy, caused by troubling the brain. Like someone in a frenzy, they think that they hear and see what other people do not, but it is all just vanity and a fantasy in their head, or else it is the result of the word of the enemy that contrives such sound in their hearing.

From *Of Angels' Song*

## The luminous darkness

You know well that the night is a space of time between two days, for when one day has ended another does not come straight away, but first comes night and separates the days, sometimes long and sometimes short, and then after that comes another day. There is also a spiritual night. You must understand that there are two days, or two lights; the first is a false light, the second is a true light. The false light is the love of this world that a person has within themselves by the corruption of the flesh; the true light is the perfect love of Jesus experienced through grace in the soul. The love of the world is a false light because it passes away and does not last, and so it does not give what it promises.

But the everlasting love of Jesus is a true day and a blessed light. For God is both love and light, and is everlasting. Therefore whoever loves God is in everlasting light. As St John says, *Qui diligit Deum manet in lumine*,[21] 'Whoever loves God lives wholly in light.' Whoever perceives and sees the love of this world as false and failing, and is therefore willing to forsake it and seek the love of God, cannot experience this divine love immediately, but must abide a while in the night, for they cannot suddenly come from the one light to the other, that is, from the love of the world to the perfect love of God. This night is nothing other than a refraining and a withdrawal of the thought of a soul from earthly things by great desire and yearning to love and see and experience Jesus and spiritual things. This is the night; for just as the night is dark, a hiding place for all physical creatures and a rest from all physical work, just so whoever intends fully to think of Jesus and to desire the love of him alone is concerned to hide their thought from vain beholding and their affection from the fleshly pleasure of all physical things, so that their thought may be free and not fixed, nor their affection bound or pained or troubled in anything beneath themselves. If they can do this, then it is night for them, for then they are in darkness.

But this is a good night and a luminous darkness, for it is a shutting out of the false love of the world, and it is an approach to the true day. In truth, the darker the night, the nearer is the true day of the love of Jesus. For the more the soul through longing for God can be hidden from the noise and din of fleshly affections and unclean thoughts, the nearer it is to experiencing the light of the love of God, for it is almost there.

Nevertheless, this night is sometimes painful and sometimes it is easy and comforting. It is painful at first for someone who is unclean and who is not through grace used to being in this darkness often.

The desire of Jesus, truly experienced in this luminous darkness, slays all stirrings of sin and enables the soul to perceive spiritual illuminations from the heavenly Jerusalem, which is Jesus.

*Scale 2*, chs 24, 25

# The soul is a mirror

It is necessary for a soul that would have knowledge of spiritual things to have first knowledge of itself. For it cannot have knowledge of a nature above itself unless it has knowledge of itself; and that is when a soul is so gathered within itself, and separated from the beholding of all earthly things and from the use of the physical senses, that it experiences itself as it is in its own nature without a body. Then if you desire to know and see what your soul is, you must not turn your thought into your body to seek it and experience it, as if it were hidden within your heart as your heart is hidden and held within the body. If you seek in this way, you shall never find it in itself; the more you seek to find and experience it as you would experience a physical thing, the further you are from it. For your soul is not a body, but an invisible life; it is not hidden and held within your body as a smaller thing is hidden and held within a larger, but holding and giving life to your body, it is much greater in power and virtue than your body is.

Then if you will find it, withdraw your thought from all physical, outward things and from consciousness of your own body also, and from all the five senses, as much as you can, and think spiritually of the nature of a rational soul, as you would think to know any virtue, such as truth or humility or any other virtue. In the same way think that a soul is a life, immortal and invisible, and has power in itself to see and know the supreme truth, and to love the supreme goodness that is God. When you see this, then you experience something of yourself. Seek yourself in no other place; but the more fully and the more clearly that you can think of the nature and the worthiness of a rational soul, what it is and what its natural activity is, the better you see yourself. It is very hard for a soul that is rude and much in the flesh to have sight and knowledge of itself thus. For when it would think of itself, or of an angel, or of God, it immediately falls into the imagination of a bodily form, and it supposes thereby to have the sight of itself, and so of God, and so of spiritual things. And that cannot be; for all spiritual things are seen and known by the understanding of the soul, not by imagination. Just as a soul sees by understanding that the virtue of justice is to give to each thing what it should have, in the same way the soul sees itself by understanding.

Nevertheless I am not saying that your soul shall rest still in this knowledge, but by this it shall seek higher knowledge above itself, that is the nature of God. For your soul is a mirror in which you shall see God spiritually. And therefore you shall first find your mirror and keep it bright and clean from fleshly filth and worldly vanity, and hold it well up from the earth, so that you may see it and in it also see our Lord; for to this end all chosen souls in this life work in their purpose and their intention, though they have not the particular experience of this. And therefore it is as I have said before, that many souls (beginning and proficient) have many great fervours and much sweetness in devotion, and, as it seems, burn completely in love, and yet they have not perfect love or spiritual knowledge of God. For understand well, however much fervour a soul experiences, even if it is so much that it thinks that the body cannot bear it, or though it completely melts into weeping, as long as its thinking and its beholding of God is mostly or all in the imagination and not in understanding, it does not yet come to perfect love or to contemplation.

For you must understand that the love of God is of three kinds. All are good, but each one is better than the one before it. The first comes only through faith, without gracious imagination or spiritual knowledge of God. This love is in the least soul that is reformed in faith, in the lowest degree of charity, and it is good because it is enough for salvation. The second love is that which a soul experiences through faith and imagination of Jesus in his humanity. This love is when the imagination is stirred by grace and it is better than the first because the spiritual eye is opened in the beholding of our Lord's humanity. The third love is that which the soul experiences through the spiritual sight of Christ's divinity in his humanity, as it may be seen here. That is best and most worthy; and that is perfect love. A soul does not experience this love until it is reformed in experience.

The prophet said thus: *Spiritus ante faciem nostram Christus Dominus, sub umbra eius vivemus inter gentes,*[22] 'Our Lord Christ is a spirit before our face; we shall live under his shadow among the nations.' That is, our Lord Jesus in his divinity is a spirit that may not be seen by us living in the flesh as he is in his blessed light. Therefore we shall live under the shadow of his humanity as long as we are here. But though this is the truth, that this love in imagination is good, nevertheless a soul should desire to have spiritual love in the understanding of the divinity, because that is the end and the full bliss of the soul, and all other physical perceptions are but means leading a soul to it. I say not that we should separate the divinity from the humanity, but we should love Jesus (both God and human, divinity in humanity and humanity in divinity) spiritually not physically.

This sight and this knowledge of Jesus, with the blessed love that comes out of it, may be called the reformation of a soul in faith and in experience of which I have spoken. It is in faith, because it is still dark compared to the full knowledge that will be had in heaven. For then we shall see not only *that* he is, but see him *as* he is; as St John says, *Tunc videbimus eum sicuti est*,[23] that is, 'Then shall we see him as he is.' Nevertheless, it is also in experience, compared with that blind knowledge which a soul has that stands in faith alone. For the soul reformed in experience knows something of the divine nature of Jesus through this gracious sight, which others do not know, but only believe to be true.

*Scale 2*, chs 30, 32

## Physical sensations

Physical experiences such as the hearing of delightful song, or the experience of comfortable heat in the body, or the seeing of light, or sweetness of physical savour are not spiritual experiences, because spiritual experiences are experienced in the powers of the soul, principally in understanding and love and little in imagination. But these feelings are in the imagination, and therefore they are not spiritual feelings. Even when they are best and most true they are but outward tokens of the inner grace that is experienced in the powers of the soul.

*Scale 2*, ch. 30

# Jesus is power, wisdom and love

*Vacate, et videte quoniam ego sum Deus,*[24] 'Cease and see that I am God.' That is, you that are reformed in experience and have your inner eye opened to the sight of spiritual things, cease from outer activity, and see that I am God. That is, see only what I, Jesus, God and human, do; look at me, for I do all. I am love, and for love I do all that I do and you do nothing. And I shall show you that this is true, for there is no good deed done in you, or good thought felt in you, unless it is done through me, that is, through power, wisdom and love, powerfully, wisely and lovingly, or else it is not a good deed. So it is true that I, Jesus, am power, wisdom and blessed love.

*Scale 2*, ch. 36

# The illumination of the Holy Spirit

When the Holy Spirit illuminates the reason into the sight of truth (how Jesus is all and that he does all), the soul has so great a love and so great a joy in that spiritual sight, because it is so true, that it forgets itself and fully leans upon Jesus with all the love that it has in order to perceive him.

The Holy Spirit as love opens the eye of the soul to the sight of Jesus, and establishes it with the pleasure of love which it experiences by that sight. It comforts the soul so powerfully that it takes no notice of what some people say or do against it, which does not weigh upon it. The most harm that it might have is the loss of that spiritual sight of Jesus.

*Scale 2*, chs 37, 38

# The opening of the spiritual eye

This opening of the spiritual eye is that luminous darkness and rich nothing of which I spoke before, and it may be called purity of spirit and spiritual rest, inward stillness and peace of conscience, highness of thought and solitude of soul, a living experience of grace and a secret of the heart, the waking sleep of the spouse and a tasting of heavenly savour, burning in love and shining in light, the entry of contemplation and reformation in experience.

*Scale 2*, ch. 40

# The hidden Christ of Holy Scripture

When the soul of a lover of Jesus experiences Jesus in prayer in the way I described earlier, and thinks that it would never experience otherwise, nevertheless it sometimes happens that grace puts a silence to vocal praying and stirs the soul to see and experience Jesus in another way. And that way is firstly to see Jesus in Holy Scripture, because Jesus, who is all truth, is hidden and concealed there, wound in soft linen under fair words, so that he may not be known or experienced except by a clean heart.

The mystery of Holy Scripture is closed under lock and key, sealed with a signet of Jesus' finger, that is, the Holy Spirit. Therefore without his love and his leave no one may come in. Only he has the key of knowledge in his keeping, as Holy Scripture says. He is the key himself, and he lets in whom he will through the inspiration of his grace, without breaking the seal. Jesus does this for his lovers, not to all alike, but to those who are specially inspired to seek truth in Holy Scripture, with great devotion in praying and with much diligence in studying preceding it. These people can come to discovery when our Lord Jesus will show it.

*Scale 2*, ch. 43

# THE *CLOUD* AUTHOR – 'THE SHARP DART OF LONGING LOVE'

The anonymous author of *The Cloud of Unknowing* wrote a series of texts on the contemplative life at roughly the same time as Hilton, that being the second half of the fourteenth century. Out of the three principal mystical writers of the fourteenth century in England the *Cloud* author is the only one who might be technically called a negative theologian, an apophatic theologian, that is, someone who stresses the essential unknowability of God.

Little, if indeed anything, is known about the *Cloud* author. It has been variously conjectured that he was a hermit, a rural priest, a Carthusian, or even a Dominican. All such biographical speculation comes from possible inferences in the author's texts that are essentially vague or ambiguous. However, the evidence as it is would suggest that he was a Carthusian.

There are a variety of influences on the *Cloud* author's teachings on contemplative prayer, but the main influences are traditions deriving from the fourth-century monk, John Cassian, and the sixth-century negative theologian, Pseudo-Dionysius the Areopagite.

Cassian's indirect influence on the *Cloud* author is one relating more to how one actually prays. As a young man Cassian joined a monastery in Bethlehem; from there he got leave to visit the saints and hermits of the Egyptian desert who taught him their way of prayer. Cassian eventually settled in southern France where he wrote his *Conferences*. St Benedict believed the *Conferences* to be such profound spiritual teaching that in his *Rule* he instructed that they were to be read by his monks. In this way the Christian spirituality of the Egyptian desert hermits had through John Cassian entered the Benedictine mainstream in the Christian West. Cassian's teaching was essentially about simplicity of intention in prayer. One was not to pray with many and various words but with a single phrase repeated over and again in pure poverty of spirit. Of this prayerful verse he writes:

> This is the verse that the mind should unceasingly cling to until, strengthened by saying it over and over again and repeating it continually, it renounces and lets go of all the abundant riches of thought. Restricting itself to the poverty of this single verse it will come easily to that first of the gospel beatitudes: for he says 'Blessed are the poor in spirit for theirs is the kingdom of heaven.'

> (*Conferences*, 10.11)

The *Cloud* author's teaching is basically a conflation of this tradition with the negative theology of Pseudo-Dionysius as developed by the Latin tradition. The *Cloud* author teaches that the contemplative must put all thoughts under a cloud of forgetting, and then in love reach out to God into the cloud of unknowing. If distracting thoughts get in the way one is silently to use a single syllable word such as 'God' or 'Love' to keep these distracting thoughts from taking one's loving attention away from God. As mentioned in the Introduction, when Dionysius' texts were translated into Latin they became augmented by influences from their now medieval theological context. Much of this development was a result of the profound influence of Bernard of Clairvaux. Principally, Dionysius' claim that God cannot be known by the intellect or by conceptual thought was supplemented by the idea that God could be reached and somehow perceived by love.[25] The idea was that God is inaccessible to reason, but accessible to love. And it is this view that is the theological basis of *The Cloud of Unknowing*, that is, that God cannot be known, but may be loved, and in that love there may be a union of the human will with the will of God. In this process the distracting and scattering effect of unruly thoughts is put under a cloud of forgetting, and in stillness one perceives God in love, without conceptual thoughts.

Although the *Cloud* author incorporates the work of Richard of St Victor into his teaching, there is a marked difference between the two in that Richard integrates the operation of reason into the process leading to contemplative union, something emphatically rejected in *The Cloud*. A free translation of Richard's *Benjamin Minor* has been ascribed to the *Cloud* author (although this ascription is doubtful), and part of it is translated in this selection. The reader will, however, notice a certain difference in contemplative approach. In many respects the teachings of *Benjamin Minor* cohere more with those of Walter Hilton.

However, there is a certain sense of development in the writings of the *Cloud* author. His teachings find a more comprehensive expression in his later work, *The Book of Private Direction*. There is here perhaps a rather more inclusive 'mysticism of being' in which contemplative union is not so restricted to the operation of the thought-free will alone. This having been said, the *Cloud* author remains a powerful exponent of negative theology, and warns us from speaking too easily about the unknown God.

We are all so very used to talking about God. We search endlessly for evocative metaphors and telling aphorisms for God. Yet God is not reducible to the linguistic source and flow of human conception and experience. This does not mean that anything goes in talking about God, but it does mean that God cannot be limited to our necessarily language-dependent conceptions. The twentieth-century theologian Austin Farrer put it like this (superbly):

When we pray, we must begin by conceiving God in full

and vigorous images, but we must go on to acknowledge the inadequacy of them and to adhere nakedly to the imageless truth of God. The crucifixion of the images in which God is first shown to us is a necessity of prayer because it is a necessity of life. The promise of God's dealing with us through grace can be set before us in nothing but images, for we have not yet experienced the reality.

When we proceed to live the promises out, the images are crucified by the reality, slowly and progressively, never completely, and not always without pain: yet the reality is better than the images. Jesus Christ clothed himself in all the images of messianic promise, and in living them out, crucified them: but the crucified reality is better than the figures of prophecy.

This is very God and life eternal, whereby the children of God are delivered from idols.[26]

*

# The four stages of the Christian life

Spiritual friend in God, you must understand well that I find, in my rough perception, four degrees or forms of Christian living, and these are: Common, Special, Solitary, and Perfect. Three of these may be begun and ended in this life, and the fourth may by grace be begun here, but it will last forever without end in the bliss of heaven. Exactly as you see that they are here put in an order, each one after the other, first Common, then Special, then Solitary, and lastly Perfect, just so I think that, in the same order and in the same course, our Lord has of his great mercy called you and led you to him by the desire of your heart.

From the first you knew well that when you were living in the common degree of Christian life in the company of your worldly friends, it seems to me, the everlasting love of the Godhead (through which God made you and fashioned you when you were nothing, and then bought you with the price of his precious blood when you were lost in Adam) would not allow you to be so far away in your form and degree of living. Therefore God graciously kindled your desire, and by it fastened a chain of longing, thereby leading you into a more special state and form of living in which you became one of his special servants. There you would learn to live more specially and more spiritually in God's service than you did or could in the common degree of living. And what more? It further seemed that God would not so lightly leave you there because of the love which God has always had for you since you came into being. And what did God do then? Do you not see how eagerly and graciously God has pulled you to the third degree and manner of living which is called Solitary? In this solitary form and manner of living you may learn to lift up the foot of your love, and step towards that state and degree of living which is perfect and the last state of all.

Look up now, you weak wretch, and see what you are! What are you and why do you deserve to be called in this way by our Lord? What a weary, wretched and slothfully sleeping heart it is that is not wakened with the attraction of his love and the voice of his calling. Beware now, wretch, at this time of your enemy, the devil, and do not regard yourself as holier or better because of the worthiness of this calling and the solitary form of living that you are in. Rather, regard yourself as even more wretched and cursed unless, by grace and direction, you do that within you which is good and which is according to your calling. Furthermore, you must be more meek and loving to your spiritual spouse, who is Almighty God, King of kings and Lord of lords, because he wishes to humble himself to such a low level as yourself, and among all the flock of his sheep graciously choose you to be one of his 'specials' and set you in the place of pasture where you may be fed with the sweetness of his love, which is a foretaste of your heritage, the kingdom of heaven.

*The Cloud*, chs 1, 2

## *The cloud of unknowing*

Lift up your heart to God with a humble stirring of love, and intend God and none of God's gifts. Hate to think of anything but God, so that nothing works in your intellect or in your will except God. To do this you must forget all created things that God ever made and their activities, so that neither your thought nor your desire are directed or extended to any of them, either generally or particularly. But let them be, and take no notice of them.

This is the work of the soul that most pleases God. All the saints and angels have joy over this work, and hasten to help it with all their power. All the devils are angry when you do it, and attempt to undermine it in every way they can. Every human living on earth is wonderfully helped by this work, more than you know. Even souls in purgatory are eased of their pain by virtue of this work. You, yourself, are cleansed and made more virtuous by this than any other work. And yet it is the lightest work of all and soonest done when a soul is helped in this sensed desire by grace, otherwise it would be extremely hard for you to do.

Therefore do not hesitate, but keep working until you experience desire. Because the first time you do it you will just find a darkness and, as it were, a cloud of unknowing, that you will not understand beyond experiencing a naked reaching out to God. Whatever you do, this darkness and this cloud is between you and God, and hinders you so that you cannot see God by the light of understanding in your reason, or experience God in the sweetness of love in your affection. Therefore prepare yourself to stay in this darkness as long as you can, continually crying out to God whom you love. For if you ever experience or see God, as far as that is possible, you will always necessarily be in this cloud and in this darkness. Yet if you work hard as I bid you, I trust in God's mercy that you will get there.

And do not think because I call it a darkness or a cloud that it is made up of the vapours of the air, nor even any darkness like that in your house at night when your candle is extinguished. Because such a darkness and such a cloud may be imagined with mental discernment as if they were before your eyes in the brightest day of summer, or even, in the darkest night of winter where you might imagine a clear shining light. Leave such misunderstanding, that is not what I mean. For when I say darkness, I mean an absence of 'knowing', as everything that you do not know or that you have forgotten is 'dark' to you, because you cannot see it with your spiritual eye. For this reason it is not called a cloud of the air, but a cloud of unknowing, which is between you and your God.

*The Cloud*, chs 3, 4

## The powers of the soul

All rational creatures, angels and humans, have each got one principal working power called a knowing power and another principal working power called a loving power. To the first power, which is a knowing power, God (the maker of them both) is forever incomprehensible, yet to the second, which is the loving power, God is fully comprehensible to each person individually. That is, one loving soul may comprehend within itself, by virtue of love, the God who is fully capable of filling every soul and angel that ever exist. This is the endless marvellous miracle of love, which shall never cease, because God will always do this and shall never cease to do it. See this, those of you who by grace can see, the experience of this is endless bliss, yet its contrary is endless pain.

Within yourself by nature are the powers of the soul, which are the three principal powers of mind, reason and will, and their secondary powers of imagination and sensuality.

There is nothing above you in nature but God.

From here on wherever you find written reference to 'yourself' in a spiritual context, you must understand by this your soul, and not your body.

The mind is such a power in itself, that properly speaking it does not itself work. But reason and will are the two working powers, as are imagination and sensuality. All these four powers and their activities are contained and comprehended within the mind. In no other sense can it be said that the mind works, unless such comprehension is an activity.

Therefore I call some powers of the mind principal powers and some secondary powers. Not that a soul is divisible, for that cannot be, but all the things in which they are active are divisible. Some are principal things, as are all spiritual things, and some are secondary, as are all physical things. The two principal working powers, reason and will, work purely in all spiritual things, without the help of the other two secondary powers. Imagination and sensuality work physically in all physical things, whether they are present or absent physically, and with the physical senses. But by them alone, without the help of reason and will, a soul can never come to know the virtue and nature of the created physical order, nor the cause of its being and its creation.

This is why reason and will are called principal powers, because they work in pure spirit without any kind of physicality; and this is why imagination and sensuality are called secondary powers, because they work in the body with bodily instruments, which are our five senses. Mind is called a principal power because it spiritually contains within itself all the other powers, and also the things on which they work.

*The Cloud*, chs 4, 62, 63

## *The cloud of forgetting*

If you ever come to this cloud, and stay and work within it as I bid you, this is what you must do. Just as there is a cloud of unknowing above you, between you and your God, in the same way put a cloud of forgetting beneath you, between you and all created things ever made. You think, perhaps, that you are far away from God because this cloud of unknowing is between you and your God. But surely, and understand this well, you are much further from God when you have not got a cloud of forgetting between you and all created things ever made. Whenever I say 'all created things ever made', I mean not only created things themselves, but their activities and situations. There are no exceptions, whether the created things are physical or spiritual, or whether their situations and activities are good or evil. In short, in this everything should be hidden under the cloud of forgetting.

For though it is fully profitable sometimes to think about certain situations and actions of particular created things, nevertheless in this work it is of little or no profit. Being mindful or thinking about anything that God ever created, or any of its actions, is a kind of spiritual light because the eye of the soul is opened to it and fixed on it, as the eye of an archer is on the target to which he shoots. But I tell you one thing, everything that you think about is above you during this time, and between you and your God. For you are far from God if anything is in your mind other than God.

Think upon the naked being of God, and love and praise God for what God is.

*The Cloud*, ch. 5

# The sharp dart of longing love

But now you ask me and say, 'How shall I think about God, and what is God?' And to this I cannot answer you apart from this, 'I do not know.'

For you have brought me with this question into that same darkness, and into that same cloud of unknowing that I wish you were in yourself. Of all creatures and their works, yes, and even of the works of God can a human, through grace have a fullness of knowing, and can reflect on them, but of God as God can no one think. And therefore I will leave all that I can think, and choose to love that of which I cannot think. Because God may well be loved, but not thought. By love God can be received and held, but by thinking never. Therefore, though it be good sometimes to think particularly of the nature and excellence of God, and although this is enlightening and a part of contemplation, nevertheless in the practice of contemplation it should be thrown down and covered with a cloud of forgetting. And you must step above it resolutely and longingly with a devout and pleasing stirring of love and strive to pierce that darkness above you. You are to smite upon that thick cloud of unknowing with a sharp dart of longing love, and do not give up for anything.

*The Cloud*, ch. 6

# The prayer of one word

If any thought rises and presses down above you between you and that darkness, and asks you saying, 'What are you looking for and what would you like to have?' say that it is God that you would have. 'God I covet, God I seek and nothing but God.' And if the thought asks you what God is, say that it is the God who made you, redeemed you, and has graciously called you to the love of God, and of whom thought can have no knowledge. Therefore say, 'Go down again,' and tread the thought down quickly with a stirring of love, even though the thought seems holy, and seems as though it would help you to seek God.

Therefore, when you decide to start this work, and feel by grace that you are called by God, lift up your heart to God with a humble stirring of love, and intend God who made you, redeemed you, and has graciously called you to this work. Do not have any thought of God, not even these, because it is enough with a naked intention direct to God, and for no other reason than God alone.

If you wish to have this intention wrapped and folded in one word, because in this way you will have a better hold of it, take but a little word of one syllable, for that is better than of two, because the shorter the word is, the better it accords with the work of the spirit. Such a word is the word 'GOD' or the word 'LOVE'. Choose which one you want, or another if you like, whichever word of one syllable you prefer. And fasten this word to your heart, so that it never leaves you whatever happens.

This word shall be your shield and your spear, whether you ride in peace or in war. With this word you shall beat on this cloud and this darkness above you. With this word you shall smite down all manner of thought under the cloud of forgetting; to the extent that if any thought presses on you to ask you what you would have, answer the thought with no more words than this one word. And if the thought offers with great learning to expound the word and tell you the associations of the word, say to the thought that you wish to have the word whole and not broken or undone. And if you hold fast to this intention, you can be sure that the thought will not remain.

Just as the short word 'FIRE' reaches and stirs its hearers quickly when it is called out, so does a short word of one syllable, not only when spoken or thought, but also when secretly meant in the depth of the spirit (which is also the height, for in the spirit all are one, height and depth, length and breadth). It reaches God more than any long psalm thoughtlessly mumbled. Therefore it is written that short prayer pierces heaven.[27]

*The Cloud*, chs 7, 37

# *The active life and the contemplative life*

You should understand well that there are two kinds of life in Holy Church. The one is active life and the other is contemplative life. Active is the lower, and contemplative is the higher. Active life has two degrees, a higher and a lower; contemplative life has also two degrees, a lower and a higher. Furthermore, these two lives are so coupled together, that though they are diverse in some areas, neither of them may be had without some part of the other. Why, the higher part of the active life is the same as the lower part of the contemplative life. So a person cannot be fully active unless they are partly contemplative, nor can a person be fully contemplative unless they are partly active. The condition of active life is such that it is both begun and ended in this life. But this is not so of contemplative life; for it is begun in this life and it shall last without end – because the part that Mary chose shall never be taken away. Active life is troubled and burdened by many things, but contemplative life sits in peace with one thing.

The lower part of the active life stands in good and honest physical works of mercy and love. The higher part of the active life and the lower part of the contemplative life lies in good spiritual mediations, and sustained perception of one's own wretchedness with sorrow and contrition, of the Passion of Christ and his servants with pity and compassion, and of the wonderful gifts, kindness and works of God in all creation, physical and spiritual, with thanksgiving and praise. But the higher part of contemplation (as it may be had here on earth) hangs totally in this darkness and in this cloud of unknowing, with a loving stirring and a blind perception of the naked being of God alone.

In the lower part of the active life a person is outside themselves and beneath themselves. In the higher part of the active life and the lower part of the contemplative life a person is within themselves and equal to themselves. But in the higher part of the contemplative life a person is above themselves and under their God. They are above themselves because they intend to come by grace where they cannot come by nature; that is, to be knit to God in spirit, and in unity of love and accordance of will.

Just as it is inconceivable to human understanding for a person to come to the higher part of the active life unless they stay for a time in the lower part, so it is that a person cannot come to the higher part of the contemplative life unless they have stayed for a time in the lower part.

*The Cloud*, ch. 8

# False contemplation

Attend humbly to this blind stirring of love in your heart. I do not mean in your physical heart, but in your spiritual heart, which is your will. Be very careful that you do not conceive physically what is meant spiritually. For I tell you truly that physical and fleshly conceptions of those who have wandering and imaginative senses are the cause of much error.

It causes a madness that comes about in this way. Some people correctly read and hear that they must leave outward working with their senses, and work inwardly. And as they do not know what inward working is, they work wrongly. This is because they direct their physical senses inwards to their bodies against the course of nature; they strain themselves as though they wanted to see inwardly with their physical eyes, and hear inwardly with their physical ears, and so forth with all their senses, of smell, of taste and of touch. In this way they reverse themselves against the course of nature, and with this inquisitiveness they work their imaginations with such lack of discernment, that they ultimately turn their brains in their heads. As soon as this happens the devil has the power to deceive them with some false light or sounds, sweet fragrances, wonderful tastes, and many strange heats and burnings in their chests or stomachs, in their backs and loins, and in their private parts.

And yet in this fantasy they think they have a tranquil consciousness of their God without any hindrance from vain thoughts. And surely, so they have in a way, because they are so filled with falsehood that worthless activity cannot harm them. And why? Because the same fiend, the devil, that would otherwise give them vain thoughts if they were in a good way, this same fiend is the chief worker of this deception. And understand well that the fiend does not hinder his own work.

Consciousness of God is not taken from these people for fear that the fiend might be suspected.

Many extraordinary expressions accompany those who are deceived in this false work (or similar forms) compared to those who are God's true disciples. God's true disciples are always controlled in their expressions, physically and spiritually. But this is not so of these others. Whoever might see them as they are during this time will see them staring wide-eyed as though they were mad, maniacally looking as though they can see the devil. They should certainly beware, for the fiend is not far away. Some of them have eyes like sheep with a brain disease that seem as though they are about to die from a blow to the head. Some hang their heads to one side as though they have a worm in their ear. Some squeak when they should speak as though there were no spirit in their bodies (and this is the normal state of hypocrites). Some cry and whine in their throats and are greedy and hasty to say what they think. And this is the condition of heretics and those who with presumption and wandering perceptions always maintain error.

I am not saying that all these unseemly expressions are great sins in themselves, nor even that those who make them are themselves great sinners. But I am saying that these unseemly and inordinate expressions govern the person who makes them, so much so that they cannot leave them when they want to. They are signs of pride and wandering perception, and of uncontrolled exhibitionism and misdirected desire for knowledge. They are true signs of instability of heart and restlessness of mind, and of ignorance of the spiritual exercises taught in this book. The only reason I detail so many of these deceptions here in this writing is so that a spiritual person may check their activity by them.

*The Cloud*, chs 51, 52, 53

# You can be called 'a God'

Whenever the mind is occupied with any physical thing, for whatever good purpose, you are, however, beneath yourself in this spiritual work, and outside your soul. Whenever you experience your mind to be occupied with the subtle conditions of the powers of the soul and their workings in spiritual things (such as your vices and virtues or those of any created being who is spiritual and equal to you in nature) in order that you might learn to know yourself in the progress to a perfect state, then you are within yourself and equal to yourself. But whenever you experience your mind occupied with nothing physical or spiritual, but with the substance of God's self alone as it is, and as it may be experienced through the work detailed in this book, then you are above yourself and under your God.

You are above yourself because you have managed to come by grace where you cannot come by nature, that is to say, to be united to God in spirit and in love and in accordance of will. Although it may be said that at this time God and you are not two but one in spirit (so much so that you or anyone who through union with God experiences the perfection of this work may, by the witness of Scripture,[28] be truly called 'a God'), you are still beneath God. For God is God by nature without beginning. You were once nothing in substance and then when you were made something by God's power and love you wilfully made yourself worse than nothing by sin. Only by God's mercy without your deserving it are you made a God in grace, united with God in spirit without separation, both here and in the bliss of heaven without end. So, although you are one with God in grace, you are, however, far beneath God in nature.

*The Cloud,* ch. 67

# The marriage of God and the soul

St Paul writes, *Qui adheret Deo, unus spiritus est cum illo.*[29] That is to say, 'Whoever draws near to God', by a reverent affection, 'is one spirit with God'; that is, although God and that person are two and distinct in nature, nevertheless in grace they are so knitted together that they are one spirit. And all this is because there is a union of love and an according of will. And in this union is the marriage made between God and the soul which shall never be broken, except by a deadly sin. In the spiritual experience of this union a loving soul may say, and sing if it wishes, that holy word written in the Song of Songs in the Bible: *Dilectus meus mihi et ego illi.*[30] That is, 'My loved one to me and I to him'; by which you must understand, 'You shall be united with the spiritual bond of grace on God's part, and the lovely consent in gladness of spirit on your part'.

From *The Epistle of Prayer*

# Benjamin

Rachel conceived by Jacob and brought forth two children. That is, reason conceived through the grace of God.

Out of reason springs right counsel, which is true discernment. This is represented by Joseph, the first son of Rachel. When we first bring forth Joseph in our reason we do all that we are stirred to do by direction. Joseph not only knows what sins we are most drawn to, but also knows the weakness of our nature. When either demand it, we find the remedy and seek counsel from those who are wiser than us, and follow their direction. Otherwise we are not Joseph, Jacob's son, born of Rachel.

By this same Joseph you are not only taught how to avoid the deceits of your enemies, but you are often also led by him to the perfect knowledge of yourself. After you have come to the knowledge of yourself, you can come to the knowledge of God, of whom you are the image and likeness. Therefore, after Joseph is Benjamin born; for as by Joseph discernment, so by Benjamin we understand contemplation. Both are born of one mother and one father. Through the grace of God enlightening our reason we come to the perfect knowledge of ourselves and of God, that is to say, as far as it may be in this life.

But it is long after Joseph that Benjamin is born; for unless we occupy ourselves thoroughly and sustainedly in spiritual work, with which we are taught to know ourselves, we cannot be raised to the knowledge and contemplation of God. It is pointless to lift your sight to the vision of God, when you cannot see yourself. Because a person must first learn to know the invisible things of their own spirit, before they presume to know the invisible things of the spirit of God. Whoever does not yet know themselves, and supposes that they have received some knowledge of the invisible things of God, I do not doubt that they are deceived. And so I advise you to seek thoroughly first to know yourself, whose soul is made in the image and likeness of God.

Know well that whoever desires to see God, it is necessary for that person to cleanse their soul, which is like a mirror in which all things may be clearly seen when it is clean. When the mirror is unclean you can see nothing clearly. This is just how it is with your soul. When it is unclean you neither know yourself, nor God. As when a candle burns, you may see the same candle by its own light, and other things too. It is the same when your soul burns in the love of God, which is when you feel your heart continually desire the love of God, then by the light of the grace which God sends to your reason you can see both your unworthiness and God's great goodness. Therefore cleanse your mirror and put your candle to the flame. Then when it is cleansed and burning, and you truly perceive this, a kind of brightness of the light of God begins to shine in your soul, and a kind of spiritual sunbeam appears in your spiritual sight, which is the eye of your soul opened to perceive God and divine realities, heaven and heavenly realities, and all manner of spiritual realities. This vision is temporary and lasts for as long as God wishes to give it to a working soul while it is in the battle of this mortal life. But after this life it will be everlasting.

Therefore, whoever wishes to come to the contemplation of God (that is to say, to give birth to the child Benjamin, which is to say, the vision of God), must do this. You must call together your thoughts and desires, and make them into a 'church', and learn therein only to love this good word 'Jesus', so that all your desire and your thought is set on loving Jesus, and that unceasingly, as far as you can here. In this way you will fulfil what is said in the psalm, 'Lord, I shall bless you in churches', that is, in the thoughts and desires of the love of Jesus. And then in this church of thoughts and desires, in this unity of studies and intentions, see that all your thoughts and desires, your studies and your intentions, are set in the loving and praising of this Lord Jesus, without forgetting, as far as you can by grace and as your frailty will allow, ever more humbling yourself to prayer and counsel, patiently abiding the will of our Lord until the time when your mind is ravished above itself to be fed with the fair food of angels in the perception of God and divine realities. So that what is written in the psalm is fulfilled: *Ibi Beniamin adolescentulus in mentis excessu*,[31] that is, 'There is Benjamin, the young child, in ravishing of mind.'

From *Benjamin Minor, The Study of Wisdom*

# St Dionysius' Prayer

Uncreated and everlasting Wisdom, you are the First Cause beyond all existence, beyond divinity, and beyond goodness, the inner supervisor of the divinely created wisdom of Christians; I beseech you to draw us up in an according power to that which is beyond the unknown and beyond the shining heights of your dark inspired speakings, where all the secret realities of theology are covered and hidden under the darkness of wisest silence that exceeds all light, making that which exceeds light to shine secretly in the utter darkness, and, in a way that is always invisible and intangible, filling with full brightness all the souls who go beyond mental vision.

For all these realities are above the mind, therefore with affection above mind, as far as I can, I desire to receive them with this prayer.

*Dionysius' Mystical Theology*, Prologue

# God who is the cause of sensible and intelligible things is none of them

Beginning with the things that are furthest away from God, we put away all things that have no substance and all things that do not exist; for these things are further away than those things that exist, but do not have life. Then we put away those things that exist, yet do not have life, for they are further away from God than those things that exist and that do have life. We then put away all those things that have life, yet lack feeling, for they are further away than those things which have feeling. We then put away those things that have feeling, yet lack reason and understanding; for they are further away than those things which have reason and understanding. And with all these things we remove from [our perception of] God all physical things, and all such things that belong to the body or to physical things, such as shape, form, quality, quantity, weight, position, visibility, sensibility, both active and passive; all the disorder of fleshly concupiscence, all the immoderation of physical passion, all the powerlessness from being subject to sensory happenings; all dependence upon light; and all generation, all corruption, all division, all capacity to suffer, and all temporal flow by the passage of time. For God is none of these things, nor has God any of them, or any other sensible things.

We also say (ascending and beginning our negations and removings with the highest of intelligible things) that God is neither soul, nor angel, neither has God imagination, nor belief, nor reason, nor understanding; neither is God reason, nor understanding; neither is God spoken, nor understood. And (going from these high things through the intermediary stages to lower things) God has no number, nor order, nor greatness, nor littleness, nor equality, nor likeness, nor unlikeness; God neither stands, nor moves, nor keeps silence, nor speaks. And (returning again to the highest things by some more intermediary stages, and ending our denyings at the highest things) we say that God has no virtue, nor is God virtue, nor light, nor does God live, nor is God life, nor substance, nor age, nor time, nor is there any intelligible contact with God, God is not knowledge, nor truth, nor kingship, nor wisdom, nor unity, nor divinity, nor goodness, nor is God spirit in the way that we understand spirit; God is neither sonhood, nor fatherhood, nor any other thing known by us or any that exist; God is not anything that comes from non-existing things, nor is God anything that comes from existing things, nor do any of these things know God as God is, nor does God know these things as they are in themselves, but only as they are in God; neither is there any way of reason or understanding to come to God, there is no name, nor knowing of God; God is not darkness, nor is God light, nor is God error, nor is God truth; nor (in summary) is there anything that we can affirm of God, nor anything that we can deny. For when we affirmingly attribute or negatingly remove all or any of the things that are not God, we cannot establish or remove God, nor in any intelligible way affirm or deny God. For the perfect and singular cause of all must necessarily be without compare of the highest height above all things, and above both affirmation and negation. And this unintelligible transcendence is, in an unintelligible way, above all affirmation and negation.

*Dionysius' Mystical Theology*, chs 4, 5

# Experiencing God through your own being

You must understand well that in this work you shall have no more perception of the qualities of God's being than of the qualities of your own being. There is no name, or experience or perception more, or as, appropriate to eternity, which is God, than that which may be had, seen, and felt in the blind and lovely perception of the word 'is'. If you say 'Good' or 'Beautiful Lord', or 'Sweet', 'Merciful' or 'Righteous', 'Wise' or 'Allknowing', 'Mighty' or 'Almighty', 'Knowledge' or 'Wisdom', 'Power' or 'Strength', 'Love' or 'Charity', or whatever else you say of God: all are hidden and stored in this little word 'is'. It is the same for God simply *to be*, as it is to be all these things. If you added a hundred thousand similarly sweet words such as these – good, beautiful and all the rest – you still would not go further that this word 'is'. If you say them all, you would not add to it, and if you said none of them, you would not diminish it. Therefore be as blind in the lovely perception of the being of your God as you are in the naked perception of your own being, without any intellectual speculation that seeks to look for any quality of God's being or of your own. Leave all such speculation well behind, and worship your God with your substance – all that you are, just as you are, worshipping all that God is, just as God is.

From *The Book of Private Direction*

## *Christ is the door and the doorkeeper*

Meditations on your sinful life, the Passion of Christ, the joys of Mary, or of all the saints and angels of heaven, or even of any quality, subtlety or characteristic that relates to the being of yourself or of God are the truest way that a person has in beginning the spiritual experience of themselves and of God. I would think that it is inconceivable to human understanding (although God can facilitate anything) that a sinner should come to rest in the spiritual experience of themselves and of God unless they first saw and experienced by imagination and meditation the earthly actions of themselves and of God, and thereby sorrowed for what they should be sorry, and were joyful for what they should enjoy. Whoever does not come in this way does not come truly; they must therefore stand outside, and they do so when they think they are well inside. For many suppose that they are inside the spiritual door, and yet they stand outside, and shall do until they humbly seek the door. There are some that soon find the door and they come in rather than other people, yet this clearly depends on the doorkeeper and not on what they might pay or deserve themselves.

The spiritual life is a marvellous household, because the Lord is not only the doorkeeper, but he is also the door. The doorkeeper he is by his divinity, and the door he is by his humanity. As he himself says in the Gospel: *Ego sum ostium. Per me si quis introierit, salvabitur; et sive egredietur sive ingredietur, pascua inveniet. Qui vero non intrat per ostium sed ascendit aliunde, ipse fur est et latro.*[32] This you should understand as if he said thus relating to our matter, 'I that am almighty by my divinity can lawfully as doorkeeper let in whomever I will, and by whatever way that I will. Yet, because I will that there be a common plain way and an open entry to all that will come, so that none be excused by ignorance of the way, I have clothed myself in the common nature of humanity, and made myself so open that I am the door by my humanity, and whoever enters by me shall be safe.'

Whoever does not enter by this door, but attempts to climb in another way to perfection by the subtle seeking and the wandering imaginations of their wild wanton senses, leaving this common plain entry and the true counsel of spiritual directors, are, whoever they are, not only a night thief but also a daylight prowler. They are a night thief because they go in the darkness of sin, presumptuously depending on their own senses and desires rather than on any true counsel or on the common plain way mentioned before. They are a daylight prowler because, under the appearance of clear spiritual living they steal the outward signs and words of contemplation, yet they have not the fruit. And therefore, because they sometimes experience a pleasant longing (however little it is) to come near God, blinded by the occurrence of this, they suppose that all that they do is good enough, when in reality it is a most dangerous direction, an immature following of the fierceness of their own desires unruled by counsel; this is especially so when their desire is singularly set on climbing to higher things, not only above themselves, but above the common plain way of Christians mentioned before, which I call, by the teaching of

Christ, the door of devotion and the truest entry to contemplation that may be had in this life.

From *The Book of Private Direction*

## *The way of contemplation*

You see both your God and your love, and nakedly experience God by spiritual union to this love in the supreme point of your spirit. You experience the inner reality of God, but blindly, as it must be in this life, utterly stripped of yourself and nakedly clothed in God as God is. You are unclothed and not wrapped in any of the sensory experiences of this life (however sweet or holy they may be). But in purity of spirit, properly and perfectly, God is perceived and experienced as God actually is, far from any fantasy or false opinion that may be held in this life.

This sight and this experience of God as God actually is can no more be separated from God (to the understanding of those who experience and see it) than the reality of God can be separated from the being of God, which are one in substance and nature. So just as the reality of God cannot be separated from the being of God because of unity in nature, so a soul that sees and experiences in this way cannot be separated from God who it sees and experiences because of unity in grace.

From *The Book of Private Direction*

# JULIAN OF NORWICH –
## 'LO ME, GODS HANDMAYD'

Julian of Norwich lived in the generation immediately following that of Walter Hilton and the *Cloud* author. On 8 May 1373, over the course of a night and the following day she received a series of sixteen visions or revelations. Sometime over the next thirty years, no one is really sure when, she wrote first a short account and then a long account of the revelations and what they had come to mean to her. Julian's text, *A Revelation of Love*,[33] remains the primary source for details of her life. Such details as there are tell us nothing specific as to Julian's theological milieu, but suggest that her revelations came to her when she was thirty and a half years old. A fifteenth-century MS tells us that Julian 'ʒit ys on lyfe anno domini millesimo ccccxiii'.

Julian was, herself, an anchoress, that is, someone who had taken vows to remain inside a particular cell for the rest of their life. Anchorites' cells were not necessarily cramped rooms, but might be a couple of rooms with a small garden. Anchorites would often have the help of servants. They would be visited by their parish priest, and they in turn would be visited by folk needing advice. Typically such folk would not actually meet the anchorite face to face, but would be spoken to through a small window on to the street. According to some contemporary wills it seems as though Julian lived to be quite old, and had a reputation for sound spiritual advice. In *The Book of Margery Kempe* Margery relates her own visit to Julian and we receive a rare glimpse of her counselling, which, although unrelated to anything she writes in *A Revelation of Love*, seems to convey her recognizable voice.

Julian's theology is rich and suggestive. She covers a great theological territory and any summary of her text would be inadequate. Over the sixteen revelations she ruminates on a variety of theological and spiritual aspects including details of Christ's crucifixion, God as Creator, humanity and love, the motherhood of Christ, sin, our substance and sensuality, and the Trinity. From a contemplative point of view Julian advocates a process of affirming reception; in many respects her model here is Mary, the mother of Jesus. She writes, '. . . in this I was taught that every contemplative soul to whom it was given to look and to seek will see Mary and pass on to God through contemplation.' In reading Julian we must always look beyond the literal sense of what she writes. On one level Julian does literally mean that we might see Mary as we 'pass on to God through contemplation', yet she also means that Mary's own receptivity to God's will must become the pattern for our own spiritual perception. Throughout Julian's *Revelation of Love*, and especially in the early chapters, Julian's own receptivity to the visions, to divine knowledge, has as its model Mary's receptivity at the Annunciation. When at the end of chapter 4 of the Long Text of the *Revelation* Julian describes Mary responding to Gabriel by saying, 'Lo me, Gods handmayd' she is simultaneously describing the response required of all Christians to God's divine action.

Julian has become rather well known over the last decade or so, yet this has been largely due to her more striking statements relating to the motherhood of Christ, or to her assuring phrase so hauntingly used in the last of T. S. Eliot's *Four Quartets*, that 'All shall be well, and all shall be well, and all manner of thing shall be well.' Incidentally, what is often forgotten about this piece of cosmic optimism is that this reassurance is only gained at the cost of the awareness of sin. Julian is not the kind of 'spiritual' person who just sees rainbows when surrounded by human suffering.

There has been a tendency in some quarters to see Julian as being a kind of proto-eco-feminist. And although liberationist theologies certainly do spring from her text, she is at the same time a woman of her age. She lived in a century that had seen plague, war, a split papacy, and religious executions (even in her home town, Norwich). She was well aware of the corrupt nature of humanity. Although she affirms the 'godly will' in each human being, she regularly refers to our 'foule, dedly flesh'. Julian's understanding of the self is a good deal more sophisticated than some popular commentators would have us believe.

What is often also missed is the strong biblical resonance within her text, especially of the writings of St Paul.[34] For example, there is much in Paul's Letter to the Romans that seems alluded to by Julian; our suffering in Christ's Passion (ch. 18) from Romans 6.3–8, the intimacy between self and God's love that nothing created can separate (ch. 46) from Romans 8.39, the relation between Adam and Christ (ch. 51) from Romans 5.12–19, and that 'all shall be well' from Romans 11.32, 36, 5.18 and 1 Corinthians 15.21–2. In *The Book of Margery Kempe* Julian cites Paul by name and quotes Romans 8.26. In many respects where Julian seems to be revolutionary, she is so *by* traditional Christian doctrine. Julian sees herself as being a teacher of Holy Church, and she is quite emphatic about this.

Where Julian differs from Hilton and the *Cloud* author is in her stress on the unity of the human soul's 'substance' and 'sensuality'. Julian moves away from a tradition which sees our sensuality (*sensualitas*) as being an aspect of our humanity that is outside the rational soul, and hence unspiritual. For Julian sensuality is unified to our spiritual substance by the union achieved by Christ in his Incarnation. As she puts it, 'Our substance and sensuality may rightly be called our soul; and that is by the union it has in God. The worshipful city that our Lord Jesus sits in is our sensuality in which he is enclosed.'

Julian is an inclusive and organic mystic. She has rightly been called an 'originist' in the sense that our spiritual union with God is in our being created by God.[35] In this she does not in essence differ from Hilton and the *Cloud* author. All three witness to the latent ability we all have for perceiving God within ourselves by virtue of our being created with a capacity for God.

*

# God is everything that is good

Our Lord showed me a spiritual sight of his homely loving. I saw that he is to us everything that is good and comforting to us. He is our clothing that wraps us, he embraces us and completely encloses us for tender love so that he will never leave us, being to us everything that is good, as to my understanding.

In this he showed a little thing, the size of a hazelnut in the palm of my hand, and it was as round as a ball. I looked at it with the eye of my understanding and thought, 'What can this be?' And the answer was, 'It is all that is made.' I marvelled at how it could continue to exist, because it seemed to me as though it could have suddenly become nothing, being so small. And I was answered in my understanding, 'It continues and always shall, because God loves it. Everything has its being by the love of God.'

In this little thing I saw three properties. The first is that God made it. The second is that God loves it, and the third, that God cares for it. But what the maker, the carer and the lover truly is I cannot tell, because until I am substantially united to God, I can never have full rest nor true bliss, that is to say, until I am so fastened to God that there is absolutely nothing that is created between God and myself.

It is necessary for us to have knowledge of the littleness of created things and to negate everything that is created to love and have God who is uncreated. For this is the reason why we are not all in ease of heart and soul, because here we seek rest in these things which are so little, and in which there is no rest, and we do not know our God who is all powerful, all wise and all good, for God is the true rest. God wishes to be known and delights that we rest in God, because everything that is beneath God is not sufficient for us, and this is the reason why no soul is rested till it is emptied of all created things. When the soul is willingly emptied for love of having God who is all, then it is able to receive spiritual rest.

'God, of your goodness, give me yourself; for you are enough for me and I cannot ask for anything that is less than full honour to you. And if I ask for anything less, I shall forever want, but only in you have I all.'

*A Revelation of Love*, ch. 5

## 'All shall be well'

Jesus answered me saying, 'Sin is inevitable, but all shall be well, and all shall be well, and all manner of thing shall be well.' In this naked word 'sin' our Lord brought generally to my mind all that is not good, the shameful despising and the utter emptying that he went through for us in this life, his dying, and all the pains and sufferings of all his creatures, spiritual and physical.

But I did not see sin, because I believe that it has no manner of substance or part of being, neither can it be known except by the pain that it causes. Therefore pain *is* something, as I understand it, for a time, because it purges us and makes us know ourselves and ask for mercy; for the Passion of our Lord is a comfort to us against all this, and so is his blessed will.

And because of the tender love that our Lord has for all that shall be saved he comforts us readily and sweetly, and means this: 'It is true that sin is the cause of all this pain, but all shall be well, and all shall be well, and all manner of thing shall be well.' These words were said very tenderly, showing no manner of blame to me for sin, nor to any that shall be saved. Therefore it was a great unkindness to blame or speculate on God for my sin, as God does not blame me for sin.

*A Revelation of Love*, ch. 27

## Prayer

Prayer is a new, gracious and lasting will of the soul united and fastened into the will of our Lord by the sweet, secret working of the Holy Spirit.

By God's grace we are made like God in our own nature, and this is the will of God, for God says, 'Pray earnestly even though you think it does not reward you experientially, for it is profitable if you do not experience it or see anything, or even if you believe that you cannot achieve anything. For in dryness and barrenness, in sickness and in feebleness, are your prayers pleasing to me, even though you think you yourself receive little experiential reward. And so is all your living prayer in my sight.'

Prayer unites the soul to God. For although the soul is like God in nature and substance, restored by grace, it is often unlike God in condition through human sin. Then is prayer a witness

that the soul wills as God wills, and it comforts the conscience
and admits us to grace. By prayer the soul accords with God.

*A Revelation of Love*, chs 41, 43

# The parable of the lord and the servant

Then our courteous Lord answered in showing very mystically
a wonderful example of a lord who has a servant.

The lord sits solemnly in rest and peace, and the servant stands
by reverently before his lord ready to do his will. The lord
looks upon his servant lovingly and sweetly, and he humbly
sends him to a certain place to do his will. The servant not only
goes, but suddenly stirs and runs in great haste for love of
doing his lord's will. And soon he falls in a valley and is badly
hurt. He then groans and moans and wails and writhes. But he
can neither rise nor help himself in any way.

The lord that sat solemnly in rest and in peace, I understood
that he is God. The servant that stood before the lord, I
understood that he represented Adam, that is to say, all
humanity.

The place that our Lord sat on was bare, a barren and desert
earth, alone in wilderness. His clothing was wide and ample as
befits a lord; the colour of his cloth was blue as azure, dignified
and beautiful. His expression was merciful, the colour of his
face was a beautiful brown with full features. His eyes were
black, most beautiful and comely, full of loving pity. And
within him was a high refuge, long and broad, full of endless
heaven. And the loving gaze with which he continually looked

upon his servant seemed to me as though it would melt our hearts for love and break them in two for joy.

His sitting on the barren and desert earth means this: he made the human soul to be his own city and his dwelling place, which is most pleasing to him of all his works; and when humanity had fallen into sorrow and pain it was not seemly for humanity to serve in that noble position. Therefore our kind Father would not prepare any other place for himself, but sits upon the earth waiting for humanity, which is mixed with earth, until the time by his grace his dear Son with his hard labour has brought his city again into its noble beauty.

In the servant is understood the Second Person of the Trinity, and in the servant is understood Adam, that is to say, all humanity. And therefore when I say 'the Son', it means the Godhead which is equal to the Father, and when I say, 'the servant', it means Christ's humanity which is truly Adam.

The lord is God the Father, the servant is the Son, Jesus Christ. The Holy Spirit is the equal love which is in them both. When Adam fell, God's Son fell because of the real union which was made in heaven. God's Son cannot be separated from Adam, because by Adam I understand humanity. Adam fell from life to death into the valley of this wretched world and after that into hell. God's Son fell with Adam into the valley of Mary's womb, who was herself the fairest daughter of Adam, in order to excuse Adam from blame in heaven and in earth, and he mightily fetched Adam out of hell.

*A Revelation of Love*, ch. 51

# Our substance and the Trinity

Because of the great, endless love that God has for all humanity, God makes no distinction in love between the blessed soul of Christ and the least soul that shall be saved. It is easy to believe and to trust that the dwelling of the blessed soul of Christ is high in the honourable divinity, and truly, as I understand in our Lord's meaning, where the blessed soul of Christ is, there is the substance of all the souls that shall be saved in Christ.

We ought to rejoice highly that God dwells in our soul, and rejoice much more highly that our soul dwells in God. Our soul is created to be God's dwelling place, and the dwelling place of the soul is God, who is uncreated.

It is a high understanding to see and know inwardly that God who is our Creator dwells in our soul; and it is a higher understanding to see and know inwardly that our soul, that is created, dwells in God's substance; of which substance, by God, we are what we are.

And I saw no difference between God and our substance, but as it were all God, and yet my understanding took it that our substance is in God, that is to say, that God is God, and our substance is a creation in God.

For the almighty truth of the Trinity is our father, for he made us and keeps us in him; and the deep wisdom of the Trinity is our mother in whom we are all enclosed; the high goodness of the Trinity is our lord and in him we are enclosed and he in us. We are enclosed in the Father, and we are enclosed in the Son, and we are enclosed in the Holy Spirit; and the Father is enclosed in us, and the Son is enclosed in us, and the Holy Spirit is enclosed in us: all power, all wisdom, all goodness, one God, one Lord.

Our faith is a virtue, a moral strength, that comes from our natural substance into our sensual soul by the Holy Spirit, and in which virtue all our virtues come to us. For without faith no one can receive virtue. Faith is nothing else than a right understanding with true belief and certain trust of our being that we are in God, and God in us, which we do not see.

And this virtue of faith (with all the others that God has ordained to us coming within it) works great things in us; for Christ's merciful working is in us, and by grace we accord to him through the gifts and virtues of the Holy Spirit, and this working makes it so that we are Christ's children and are Christian in living.

*A Revelation of Love*, ch. 54

# Our substance is in God and God is in our sensuality

I saw that our substance is in God, and I also saw that God is in our sensuality; for at the self-same point that our soul is made sensual, at the same point it is the eternal city of God, into which God comes and from which God will never leave, for God is never out of the soul and dwells within it blissfully without end.

God is nearer to us than our own soul, because God is the ground in whom our soul stands and God is the mean(s) that keeps our substance and our sensuality together so that they shall never be separated. Our soul sits in God in true rest and our soul stands in God in true strength and our soul is rooted by its nature in God in endless love. And therefore if we desire to have knowledge of our soul and enjoy inner relationship, it is necessary to seek into our Lord God in whom it is enclosed.

And regarding our substance and sensuality, it may rightly be called our soul; and that is by the union it has in God.

The honourable city that our Lord Jesus sits in is our sensuality in which he is enclosed, and our natural substance is enclosed in Jesus whose own blessed soul sits at rest in the Godhead.

We can never come to full knowledge of God until we first clearly know our own soul; for until the time it is in its full powers we cannot be fully holy, and that is when by the virtue of Christ's Passion our sensuality is brought up to the substance.

In Christ our two natures are united; for the Trinity is comprehended in Christ in whom our higher part is grounded and rooted, and he has also taken our lower part, which nature was first ordained to him.

*A Revelation of Love*, chs 55, 56, 57

## Christ is our mother

Our high Father, God almighty, who is Being, knew us and loved us before all time. From this knowledge, in marvellous deep love, and through the foreseeing endless communication of the blessed Trinity, God wished that the Second Person should become our mother, our brother and our saviour. It therefore follows that, as truly as God is our father, as truly God is our mother.

Thus Jesus is our true mother in nature from our creation, and he is our true mother in grace through taking our created nature.

A mother may feed her child with her milk, but our precious mother Jesus may feed us with himself, this he does most courteously and most tenderly with the blessed sacrament that is the precious food of true life.

A mother may lean her child tenderly to her breast, but our tender mother Jesus may intimately lead us into his blessed breast through his sweet open side, and show us there some of the Godhead and the joys of heaven with endlessly blissful spiritual sureness.

This fair and lovely word 'mother' is so sweet and so of the very nature of the self that it may not be truly said of anyone but of Christ (and of her who is his mother and ours). To the property of motherhood belongs natural love, wisdom and knowledge, and it is good. Although our physical birth is little, low and simple with regard to our spiritual birth, Jesus is actively present when mothers give birth.

*A Revelation of Love*, chs 59, 60

# *The soul is a beautiful child*

At this time I saw a body lying on the ground which seemed heavy and ugly, without shape and form as if it were a swollen quag of stinking mire. And suddenly out of this body sprang a beautiful creature, a little child fully shaped and formed, swift and lively, whiter than a lily, which swiftly glided up to heaven. And the swollenness of the body signified the great wretchedness of our mortal flesh, and the littleness of the child signified the clean purity of the soul. And I thought, 'With this body there is none of the child's beauty, nor on this child is there any of the foulness of the body.'

*A Revelation of Love*, ch. 64

# The soul is an endless city

Then our Lord opened my spiritual eye and showed me my soul in the midst of my heart. I saw the soul to be so large as if it were an endless world and as if it were a blissful kingdom; and by the conditions I saw within it I understood that it is an honourable city. In the midst of that city sits our Lord Jesus, God and human, a beautiful person and of great stature, the highest bishop, the most solemn king, the most honourable lord, and I saw him clothed solemnly and honourably. He sits in the soul righteously in peace and rest. And the Godhead rules and takes care of heaven and earth and all that is, being sovereign power, sovereign wisdom and sovereign goodness.

The place that Jesus takes in our soul he shall never leave without end as to my sight; for in us is his most intimate home and his endless dwelling. And in this he showed me the delight that he had in the creation of the human soul.

And therefore the blessed Trinity eternally enjoys the creation of the human soul; for our Lord saw from without beginning what would delight him without end.

In the human soul is God's true dwelling; and the highest light and the brightest radiance of the city is the glorious love of our Lord.

*A Revelation of Love*, ch. 67

# Three things

There are three things by which humans stand in this life. And by these three things God is worshipped and we are furthered, looked after, and saved. The first is the use of natural, human reason, the second is the teaching of Holy Church, and the third is the inner gracious working of the Holy Spirit, and these three come from one God. God is the ground of our natural reason, God is the teaching of Holy Church, and God is the Holy Spirit. All are different gifts to which God wants us to show great regard and attention. They work continually within us and are great things. Of these great things God wishes us to have knowledge as in an 'ABC', that is to say, that we have a little knowledge here of the complete knowledge we shall have in heaven, and this is to further us.

*A Revelation of Love*, ch. 80

# Jesus lives in the city of the soul

Our good Lord showed himself in several ways, both in heaven and on earth, but I saw him take no place but in our own soul. He showed himself on earth in the sweet Incarnation and in his blessed Passion. And in another way he showed himself on earth when I said earlier, 'I saw God in a point.' In a further way he showed himself on earth as if on pilgrimage, that is to say, he is here with us, leading us, and shall be until he has brought us all to his bliss in heaven. He showed himself at different times reigning, as I have already said, but principally in the human soul. He has taken the soul as his resting place and his honourable city, and out of this honourable place he shall never rise or leave. Marvellous and splendid is this place where the Lord dwells. And therefore he wants us to attend readily to his gracious touching, more enjoying ourselves in his complete love, than sorrowing in our frequent failings. For the greatest honour to him of anything that we can do is that we live gladly and happily, because of his love, in our penance. He watches us so tenderly that he sees all our living and penance, and natural love for him is the same as eternal penance in us.

*A Revelation of Love*, ch. 81

## 'Love was his meaning'

This book is begun by God's gift and his grace, but it is not yet performed, as to my sight.

From the time that it was revealed I often desired to understand what was our Lord's meaning. And fifteen years and more afterwards I was answered in spiritual understanding, saying thus: 'Would you understand your Lord's meaning in this thing? Understand it well, love was his meaning. Who showed it to you? Love. What did he show you? Love. Why did he show it? For love. Hold yourself therein and you shall understand and know more of the same; but you shall never know nor understand anything else therein ever.' Thus was I taught that love was our Lord's meaning.

*A Revelation of Love*, ch. 86

# PARAMYSTICAL WRITINGS

This last section is a collection of passages from texts written both before and after those of Hilton, the *Cloud* author and Julian. They are not all necessarily 'mystical' texts in the sense that they deal with contemplation proper, what Hilton would call 'very contemplacion', which is the knowledge and perfect love of God found in the union of the soul with Christ. The passages from Richard Rolle and Margery Kempe reveal an interest in devotional phenomena which are not contemplation as such. The great mystical teachers of the Church have always taught that such physical responses are potentially distracting and are not to be sought. As Mother Mary Clare SLG writes on the great Teresa of Avila:

> In the chapters on the Fifth Mansion of *The Interior Castle* Teresa is at great pains to remind us that many outward signs in the life of prayer that appear to some as marvels – visions, locutions, raptures, the gift of tears – (I wonder what she would think of today's gift of tongues!) are by-products of the spiritual graces that the soul is not strong enough to receive. To the saint they are an elementary stage of spiritual development albeit for some, perhaps, a neces-sary one.[36]

The passages in this last section are thus grouped under the heading 'Paramystical Writings', that is, writings associated with practices that may be found 'on the boundaries between mysticism and devotion'.[37]

The first passage is taken from the guide for anchoresses

entitled *Ancrene Wisse* (or often *Ancrene Riwle*). This text, first written in the early thirteenth century by a chaplain to three sisters, was a well-known manual of devotion for anchoresses and was widely used and copied well into the following century and much traditional theological and spiritual teaching was imparted to its readers. The translated passage conveys the Augustinian Trinitarian teaching that so pervaded the writings of the fourteenth-century mystics.

The second pair of passages are taken from St Edmund of Abingdon's *Mirror of the Church* (*Speculum Ecclesiae*). Edmund of Abingdon, or Edmund Rich, became Archbishop of Canterbury in 1233 and his highly influential text is found in French, Latin, and English MSS. The *Mirror of the Church* was particularly noted and used for its meditations on Christ's Passion. However, the two translated passages here both relate to contemplation; the first relates to the 'acquired' contemplation of created things and of Holy Scripture, the second relates to the higher 'infused' contemplation of God in the soul.

The rest of this section is devoted to Richard Rolle and Margery Kempe. Rolle was particularly influential in the fourteenth century and had a good number of followers even after his death. His grave at Hampole Priory in South Yorkshire became a site of pilgrimage. It is almost certain that both Hilton and the *Cloud* author have Rolle's followers in mind when they write about the dangers of extreme, physical mannerisms indulged in by some who are attempting to follow the spiritual life.

Rolle was born in Yorkshire around 1300 and died in 1349. As a young man he went to study at Oxford. However, he clearly found life difficult there and he returned to Yorkshire at the age of 19 to lead the life of a hermit with a self-made grey and white habit adapted from two of his sister's dresses. In Rolle's book *The Fire of Love* (*Incendium Amoris*) he is scathing about formal theologians suggesting that they have no idea what the love of God is. And it was to the love of God and its delights that Rolle was to apply himself throughout his life. Rolle was intensely Christocentric, writing vivid meditations on Christ's Passion, and he is particularly noted for his devotion to the Name of Jesus. He was especially interested in the life of recluses and wrote as a spiritual director, most notably to a Margaret de Kirkeby, to whom he addressed his book, *The Form of Living*, which dealt with the spiritual regime of the solitary life. Rolle and she were great friends and it is likely that other English texts of his were written for her.

Benedicta Ward SLG summarizes Rolle well when she writes, 'Rolle was not a theologian nor a theorist, and while as a mystical theology his work is certainly limited and incomplete, as a record of personal experience it is both sensitive and lucid.'[38]

The final selections are from *The Book of Margery Kempe*. The *Book* is an account of Margery's life from the time of her marriage in 1393 onwards. She was born around 1373 and died sometime after 1438. Her life and particularly her histrionic behaviour aroused much controversy around her. She caused significant irritation to those who witnessed her public screaming, her 'crying and roaring'. She in turn felt people to be unjustly cruel, and in many respects her life is a sad one. She herself details a bout of insanity and more than one commentator has suggested that rather more of her behaviour was the result of psychiatric illness.

This having been said, the *Book* gives us a vivid narrative of her life and travels. Her home was King's Lynn and she was a (proud) mother of fourteen children, yet following a call to celibacy to which her husband conceded in her thirties she travelled widely around the country and made pilgrimages to Jerusalem, to Assisi and Rome (where she experienced a spiritual marriage to the Godhead), and to Compostela.

The *Book* was written for her by a friendly priest who had to copy a very poorly written draft made by an earlier scribe. In many respects it reads like a defence of her life. It has not been received overly well for its theological merit. David Knowles writes that her work 'has little in it of deep spiritual wisdom, and nothing of true mystical experience.'[39] Although some readers may well be quickly driven to irritation with Margery, the *Book* offers us some remarkable glimpses of the religious life and times following the great fourteenth-century mystics.

# *Ancrene*  (A Guide for Anchoresses)

## *Prayer to the Trinity*

Almighty God, Father, Son, and Holy Spirit, as you three are one God, so you are one power, one wisdom, and one love, and yet in Holy Scripture power is especially attributed to you, dearest Father, wisdom to you, good Son, love to you, Holy Spirit; one almighty God, threefold in three Persons, give me these same three things, power to serve you, wisdom to please you, love and will to do it, power that I may do it, wisdom that I may know how to do it, love that I may desire to do always that which you love. As you are full of every good, and there is no good that is absent where these three are present, power, wisdom, and love joined together, pour out these to me, Holy Trinity, in your own honour.

From *Ancrene Wisse*, Part 1

# St Edmund of Abingdon

## *Contemplation of created things and of Holy Scripture*

There are three kinds of contemplation. The first is contemplation of created things, the second is of Holy Scripture, and the third is of God's self and God's nature. Contemplation is nothing other than the sight of God.

There are three things in God: Power, Wisdom, and Goodness. Power is attributed to God the Father, Wisdom to God the Son, and Goodness to God the Holy Spirit. Through God's Power all things were formed, through God's Wisdom all things were wonderfully ordained, and through God's Goodness all things are multiplied every day.

Say to your Lord therefore in your heart: 'Because you exist all things do; because you are beautiful all things are beautiful; because you are good all things are good. All created things honour you with good reason, they praise you, they glorify you in what they do, blessed God in Trinity! Of whose power are all things created; of whose wisdom are all things governed; and of whose bounty are all things multiplied, to whom be honour and glory, world without end. Amen.'

The second degree of contemplation is in Holy Scripture. But now you, who have little learning, will ask me, 'In what way can I ever come to the contemplation of Holy Scripture?'

Now understand, I will tell you. If you cannot understand what is written, listen to the good things that people say from

Scripture. When you hear anything from Scripture in a public sermon or in a private conversation, take heed immediately if you hear anything that may help you in edification.

Take heed of what you should do and how you should live, and everything that may illuminate your understanding in the knowledge of truth, and warm your will and affection in the heat of love. Everything that is written in Holy Scripture, whether hidden or open, deals with these two good things.

From *The Mirror of the Church*

## Contemplation in the soul

A person comes first to the knowledge of their Creator, how God is without beginning and is called God, one in substance and three in persons, and why the first person is called God the Father, the second the Son, and the third the Holy Spirit. In this way you shall know your God. Such a way of knowing is the foundation of contemplation. And therefore, when you have in this way established your heart in right faith, and steadfast hope, and perfect love, then you shall lift up your heart in high contemplation of your Creator. Through contemplation the soul would like to see God in God's own nature, but it cannot do it. So it turns to its own stages of ascent by which it may climb to the contemplation of God, first by seeing and knowing its own nature, and after that the nature that is above it. But if your thought is fragmented through worldly thoughts, it can never properly seek God, nor God's nature. And why is this? It is because the foul thoughts which lead the soul become obstacles.

The first degree of this way of contemplation is when the soul turns to itself and gathers itself fully within itself. The second degree is when the soul sees its nature when so gathered together. The third degree is when the soul lifts itself above itself and strives to see God its Creator in God's own nature.

However, the soul can never turn to itself until it has learned to stand against and repel all kinds of physical, worldly or heavenly imagination; everything that comes to one's heart from sight, hearing, touch, smell or from any physical sense must be subdued so that the soul can see itself as it is without the body.

Think how great the soul is, that with one thought can comprehend heaven and earth and everything in them, even if they were a thousand times greater than they are. If the human soul is so great and so noble that no creature can perfectly understand it, how great and how noble is our God who created such a noble thing out of nothing! So great: God is above all things and beneath all things, God is within all things and without all things. God is above all things, governing them; God is beneath all things, sustaining them; within all things, fulfilling them; without all things, surrounding them. Such contemplation engenders steadfast belief and true devotion.

From *The Mirror of the Church*

# Richard Rolle

## *The heart on fire*

I marvelled more than I can show when I first felt my heart grow warm, and it was a real warmth too, not imagined, but as if it burned with physical fire. I was amazed as the burning in my soul burst out with an unexpected consolation. Out of ignorance of such healing abundance I often touched my chest, seeking whether this burning was caused by any outward physical cause. But when I knew it was kindled by an inward spiritual cause alone, and that this burning was not from fleshly love or concupiscence, I realized that it was the gift of my Maker. Therefore I melted into the desire of greater love, and especially for the inflowing of the most sweet longing and spiritual pleasure which comforted my mind with spiritual flames. Before experiencing all this comforting heat and being filled with devotional pleasure, I believed that no one could experience such heat in this exile of ours, for truly, it so enflames the soul it is as if the element of fire were burning there.

*The Fire of Love*, Prologue

## *Heat, song, and sweetness*

Seeking in Scripture I find that the highest love of Christ is found in three things: in heat, in song, and in sweetness. And these three, as I know from experience, cannot be received except by great stillness.

I call it heat when the mind is truly kindled in everlasting love, and the heart in the same manner burns in a way that is truly felt. The heart when truly turned into flames gives an experience of burning love.

I call it song when an overflowing soul receives the warming sweetness of everlasting loving, thought is turned into song, and the mind is transformed by the sweetest sound.

These two experiences are not gained through idleness, but by the highest devotion. From these two comes the third, which is to say, unbelievable sweetness. Heat and song cause an amazing sweetness in the soul, and of a great sweetness they themselves can also be caused.

*The Fire of Love*, Bk 1, ch. 15

## *Spiritual song*

O sweet Jesus, I bind your love in me with a knot that cannot be untied, seeking the treasure that I desire, and I find a longing, because in you I do not cease to thirst. Therefore my sorrow vanishes like the wind, for my reward is a spiritual song which no one hears. My inward nature is turned into sweet song, and for love I long to die.

While these things come that take me, and taking me refresh me, a dazzling greatness of gifts delights me and lingering love punishes me with joy.

*The Fire of Love*, Bk 2, ch. 8

# Margery Kempe

## *Margery visits Julian*

Margery was bidden by our Lord to go to an anchoress in the same city who was called Dame Julian. So she did and showed her the grace that God had put in her soul of compunction, contrition, sweetness and devotion, compassion with holy meditation and high contemplation, the very many holy speeches and light conversations which our Lord had given her soul, and the many wonderful revelations, which she showed to the anchoress to know if there were any deception in them, because the anchoress was expert in such things and could give good counsel.

The anchoress, hearing the marvellous goodness of our Lord, highly thanked God with all her heart for such visitations to Margery, counselling her to be obedient to the will of our Lord God and to fulfil with all her power whatever was so put in her soul if it were not against the worship of God or the profit of her fellow Christians. For if it were, then it was not the actions of a good spirit, but rather of an evil spirit.

'The Holy Spirit never moves anything against love, and if it did, it would be against its own self, which is all love. Also the Holy Spirit moves a soul to chastity, for chaste livers are called the temple of the Holy Spirit.[40] The Holy Spirit makes a soul stable and steadfast in the right faith and the right belief.

'A person with a duplicitous soul is forever unstable and unsteadfast in all their ways. Whoever is always doubting is like a wave of the sea that is moved and borne about by the wind, and such a person is not likely to receive the gifts of God.[41]

'Whoever has the good tokens must steadfastly believe that

the Holy Spirit dwells in their soul. And much more, when God visits a person with tears of contrition, devotion, or compassion, they can and ought to believe that the Holy Spirit is in their soul. St Paul says that the Holy Spirit asks for us with unspeakable mournings and weepings.[42] That is to say, the Holy Spirit makes us ask and pray with such plentiful mournings and weepings that the tears cannot be numbered. No evil spirit can give these tokens, for St Jerome says that tears torment the devil more than the pains of hell. God and the devil are forever against each other, and they shall never dwell together in one place, and the devil has no power in a person's soul.

'Holy Scripture says that the soul of a righteous person is the seat of God,[43] and so I trust, sister, that you are. I pray God grant you perseverance. Set all your trust in God and do not fear the language of the world, for the more spite, shame and reproof that you have in the world, the more is your merit in the sight of God. It is necessary for you to have patience, for in that shall you keep your soul.'

Great was the holy conversation that the anchoress and this creature had by communing in the love of our Lord Jesus Christ the many days that they were together.

*The Book of Margery Kempe*, Bk 1, ch. 18

# In Jerusalem Margery has a vision of Christ

They went to the Church of the Holy Sepulchre in Jerusalem and they were let in on the one day at the time of evensong and they stayed inside until the time of evensong on the following day. Then the friars lifted up a cross and led the pilgrims about from one place to another where our Lord had suffered his pains and his passions, every man and woman bearing a wax candle in their hand. And the friars always, as they went about, told them what our Lord suffered in every place. And the aforementioned creature, Margery, wept and sobbed so plenteously as though she had seen our Lord with her bodily eyes suffering his Passion at that time. Before her in her soul she saw him truly by contemplation, and that caused her to have compassion.

When they came up on to the Mount of Calvary, she fell down because she could not stand or kneel, but writhed and wrestled with her body, spreading her arms wide, and cried with a loud voice as though her heart should break, for in the city of her soul she saw truly and freshly how our Lord was crucified. Before her face she heard and saw in her spiritual sight the mourning of our Lady, of St John and Mary Magdalen, and of many others that loved our Lord. And she had such great compassion and such great pain in seeing our Lord's pain that she could not keep herself from crying and roaring. This was the first cry that she ever cried in contemplation. And this kind of crying endured for many years after this time, despite what anyone could do, and therefore she suffered much spite and reproof. The crying was so loud and so incredible that people were astounded, unless they had heard it before, or else knew the cause of the crying. And she cried so often that she was made quite weak in her physical powers, and especially if she heard of our Lord's Passion.

*The Book of Margery Kempe*, Bk 1, ch. 28

## Margery prays about her tears

Lord, the world cannot allow me to do your will or follow your stirrings. I therefore pray that, if it is your will, take away this crying from me at the time of sermons so that I do not cry at your holy preaching. Let me have them by myself alone so that

I am not removed from hearing your holy preaching and your holy word. For there is no greater pain that I could suffer in this world than to be removed from hearing your holy word. If I were in prison, my greatest pain would be the deprivation of your holy word and of your holy sermons. And, good Lord, if you still wish me to cry, I pray that you give me this crying when I am alone in my room as much as ever you will and spare me among the people, if it please you.

*The Book of Margery Kempe*, Bk 1, ch. 77

# The marital union of the soul with Christ

When Margery saw weddings, men and women being joined together following the law of the Church, she then had in meditation how our Lady was joined to St Joseph, and of the spiritual joining of the soul to Jesus Christ. She prayed to our Lord that her love and affection might be joined to him alone without end, and that she might have the grace to obey him, love and dread him, honour and praise him, love nothing but what he loved, desire nothing but what he desired, and always be ready to fulfil his will both night and day without grumbling or depression, with complete gladness of spirit. And she had many more holy thoughts than she could ever repeat, and she did not receive these through her own study or intellect, but of his gift whose wisdom is incomprehensible to all creatures, except to those alone whom he chooses and illumines as he himself wills. For his will may not be constrained, it is in his own free disposition.

*The Book of Margery Kempe*, Bk 1, ch. 82

# Margery's final prayer

I bless my God in my soul and all you that are in heaven.
Blessed may God be in you all and you all in God. Blessed be
you, Lord, for all your mercies that you have shown to all that
are in heaven and on earth. And I especially bless you, Lord,
for Mary Magdalen, for Mary of Egypt, for St Paul, and for St
Augustine. As you have shown mercy to them, so show your
mercy to me and to all who heartily ask for mercy. The peace
and the rest which you have bequeathed to your disciples and
to your lovers, bequeath the same peace and rest to me on
earth and in heaven without end.

*The Book of Margery Kempe*, Prayers of the Creature

# Notes

1. I would like to thank Professors Michael Sargent, Stan Hussey, and Toshiyuki Takamiya for their kindness in making Middle English texts of Hilton's *Scale of Perfection* and *Of Angels' Song* available to me.
2. See Rowan Williams' ' "Know Thyself": What Kind of an Injunction?' in McGhee (ed.) *Philosophy, Religion, and the Spiritual Life*, 1992, p. 216.
3. '*Noverim me, noverim te*' (*Soliliquies* 2.1.1).
4. *De Spiritu et Anima*, ch. 52.
5. This Augustinian triad remained influential and is used in the definition of the Trinity in Article I of the Thirty-Nine Articles of the Church of England: 'There is but one living and true God, everlasting, without body, parts, or passions; of infinite power, wisdom, and goodness; . . .'
6. 'But it is not the spiritual that is first, but the physical, and then the spiritual' (1 Corinthians 15.46).
7. The seven physical deeds of mercy were to feed the hungry, give drink to the thirsty, clothe the naked, give lodging to the stranger, visit the sick, visit prisoners, and bury the dead (see Matthew 25.34–46). The seven spiritual deeds of mercy were to convert the sinner, instruct the ignorant, counsel the doubting, comfort the grieving, bear wrongs patiently, forgive injuries, and pray for the living and the dead.
8. 'Anyone united to the Lord becomes one spirit with him' (1 Corinthians 6.17, all footnoted biblical quotations in English are from the NRSV Anglicized Edition).
9. 'For if I pray in a tongue, my spirit prays but my mind is unproductive. What should I do then? I will pray with the spirit, but I will pray with the mind also; I will sing praise with the spirit, but I will sing praise with the mind also' (1 Corinthians 14.14–15).
10. 'The fire on the altar shall be kept burning; it shall not go out. Every morning the priest shall add wood to it, lay out the burnt offering on it, and turn into smoke the fat pieces of the offerings of well-being. A perpetual fire shall be kept burning on the altar; it shall not go out' (Leviticus 6.12–13).
11. Hilton here refers to Bernard of Clairvaux's notion of '*carnalis amor Christi*' (*In Cant.* 20).
12. 'For I decided to know nothing among you except Jesus Christ, and him crucified' (1 Corinthians 2.2).

13. 'May I never boast of anything except the cross of our Lord Jesus Christ' (Galatians 6.14).

14. From 'But we proclaim Christ crucified, a stumbling block to Jews and foolishness to Gentiles, but to those who are the called, both Jews and Greeks, Christ the power of God and the wisdom of God' (1 Corinthians 1.23–4).

15. 'Mary has chosen the better part, which will not be taken away from her' (Luke 10.42). In the Christian contemplative tradition and generally, Mary Magdalen (Luke 8.2), Mary of Bethany (John 11.1–6) and the woman who was a sinner (Luke 7.37) were understood as being the same person.

16. 'Every place on which you set foot shall be yours' (Deuteronomy 11.24).

17. 'Your word is a lamp to my feet' (Psalm 119.105).

18. 'The eye is the lamp of the body' (Matthew 6.22).

19. 'My little children, for whom I am again in the pain of childbirth until Christ is formed in you' (Galatians 4.19).

20. 'No one comes to the Father except through me' (John 14.6).

21. From 'Whoever loves a brother or sister lives in the light' (1 John 2.10).

22. From 'The Lord's anointed, the breath of our life, was taken in their pits – the one of whom we said, "Under his shadow we shall live among the nations" ' (Lamentations 4.20).

23. From 'Beloved, we are God's children now; what we will be has not yet been revealed. What we do know is this: when he is revealed, we will be like him, for we will see him as he is' (1 John 3.2).

24. 'Be still, and know that I am God' (Psalm 46.10).

25. Again, see Bernard McGinn's 'Love, Knowledge, and Mystical Union in Western Christianity: Twelfth to Sixteenth Centuries', *Church History* 56, 1987, pp. 7–24.

26. In 'Rudolph Bultmann: An English Appreciation', *Kerygma and Myth: A Theological Debate*, Vol. 1, ed. Bartsch, trans. Fuller, SPCK, 1964.

27. 'The prayer of the humble pierces the clouds' (Ecclesiasticus 35.17).

28. 'Jesus answered, "Is it not written in your law, 'I said, you are gods'? . . . those to whom the word of God came were called 'gods' – and the scripture cannot be annulled" ' (John 10.34, 35). There is also very likely influence here from William of St Thierry's *Golden Epistle*.

29. 'Anyone united to the Lord becomes one spirit with him' (1 Corinthians 6.17).

30. 'My beloved is mine and I am his' (Song of Songs 2.16).
31. 'There is Benjamin, the youth, in ecstasy of mind' – a Vulgate reading derived from 'There is Benjamin, the least of them, in the lead' (Psalm 68.27 (Psalm 67.28 Vulgate)).
32. 'I am the gate. Whoever enters by me will be saved, and will come in and go out and find pasture.' 'Anyone who does not enter the sheepfold by the gate but climbs in by another way is a thief and a bandit' (John 10.9, 1).
33. As stated earlier, the singular designation 'A Revelation of Love' is that of Julian's text (in all MSS of the Long Text) and is to be preferred. See Introduction, note 2.
34. Denise Nowakowski Baker also identifies possible influence of Romans on Julian, particularly on the subject of justification. See Baker, 1994, p. 111f. Bernard McGinn has written that 'Julian was the most Pauline of the fourteenth-century mystics', *Christian Spirituality*, Vol. 2, (ed. Jill Raitt), London, SCM Press, 1989, p. 203.
35. See *A Lesson of Love*, John-Julian OJN, 1988, p. vii.
36. *Carmelite Ascent*, SLG Press, 1973, p. 7.
37. See Hirsh, 1989, p. 19.
38. Wakefield (ed.), 1983, p. 336.
39. Knowles, 1961, p. 148. For a fine recent, and positive, appraisal, see Santha Bhattacharji's *God is an Earthquake*, 1997.
40. 1 Corinthians 6.19.
41. James 1.6–8.
42. Romans 8.26.
43. 2 Corinthians 6.16.

# Select Bibliography

There has been a marked increase in publications on the English Mystics in recent years. Unfortunately, at the more popular end many of these publications rest on dubious scholarship and have rather misrepresented the teachings of the mystics. In this select bibliography I have listed only work based on sound learning.

Similarly, translations of the English Mystics vary in quality. All those listed below are good, the best being: the Clark and Dorward translation of Hilton, the Walsh translations of the *Cloud* author, and John-Julian's translation of Julian. Something of Julian is lost in translation, and readers should be encouraged to try the Middle English text for themselves. The Glasscoe edition of *A Revelation of Love* should be used as it is based on the best manuscripts. The introductions and notes to all of these editions are highly recommended.

The best recent studies on the English Mystics are those contained in *The Medieval Mystical Tradition in England*, Volumes I–V, edited by Marion Glasscoe. Her own general book, *English Medieval Mystics*, is also especially good. Particular commendation should also be made of the work of Vincent Gillespie, Denise Nowakowski Baker, Joan Nuth, and Nicholas Watson.

## WALTER HILTON

*Texts*

*The Scale of Perfection, Book 1*, Cambridge University Library Additional MS 6686 corrected by other MSS, ed. Michael Sargent, Early English Text Society (EETS), Oxford University Press, (forthcoming).

*The Scale of Perfection, Book 2,* British Library MS Harley 6579 corrected by other MSS, ed. S. S. Hussey, EETS, Oxford University Press, (forthcoming).

*Mixed Life,* ed. from MS Lambeth Palace 472, ed. S. J. Ogilvie-Thomson, Elizabethan and Renaissance Studies 92:15, Universität Salzburg, 1986.

*Two Minor Works of Walter Hilton: Eight Chapters on Perfection and Of Angels' Song,* ed. Fumio Kuriyagawa and Toshiyuki Takamiya, Tokyo, privately printed, 1980.

*Translations*

*Walter Hilton: The Scale of Perfection,* trans. and with an Introduction by John P. H. Clark and Rosemary Dorward, *Classics of Western Spirituality (CWS),* New York, Paulist Press, 1991.

*The Stairway of Perfection,* trans. M. L. del Mastro, New York, Doubleday, 1979.

*The Ladder of Perfection,* trans. Leo Sherley-Price, Harmondsworth, Penguin, 1957.

*Minor Works of Walter Hilton,* ed. Dorothy Jones, London, Burns, Oates and Washbourne Ltd, 1929.

*Eight Chapters on Perfection and Of Angels' Song,* trans. Rosemary Dorward, Oxford, SLG Press, 1983.

## THE *CLOUD* AUTHOR

*Texts*

*The Cloud of Unknowing and Related Treatises,* ed. Phyllis Hodgson, *Analecta Cartusiana* 3, Universität Salzburg, 1982.

The Cloud of Unknowing and The Book of Privy Counselling, ed. Phyllis Hodgson, EETS (OS 218), Oxford University Press, 1944.

Deonise Hid Divinity and Other Treatises on Contemplative Prayer Related to The Cloud of Unknowing, A Tretyse of the Stodye of Wysdome that Men Clepen Beniamyn, A Pistle of Preier, A Pistle of Discrecioun of Stirrings, A Tretis of Discrescyon of Spirites, ed. Phyllis Hodgson, EETS (OS 231), Oxford University Press, 1955.

## Translations

The Cloud of Unknowing and The Book of Privy Counseling, ed. William Johnson, New York, Doubleday, 1973.

The Cloud of Unknowing, trans. James Walsh, CWS, New York, Paulist Press, 1981.

The Pursuit of Wisdom and Other Works by the Author of The Cloud of Unknowing, trans. James Walsh, CWS, New York, Paulist Press, 1988.

The Cloud of Unknowing and Other Works, ed. Clifton Wolters, Harmondsworth, Penguin, 1961.

A Study of Wisdom: Three Tracts by the Author of The Cloud of Unknowing, trans. Clifton Wolters, Oxford, SLG Press, 1980.

## JULIAN OF NORWICH

### Texts

Julian of Norwich's Revelations of Divine Love, (Short Text) ed. Frances Beer, Middle English Texts 8, Heidelberg, 1978.

A Book of Showings to the Anchoress Julian of Norwich, 2 Vols,

(Paris MS) ed. Edmund Colledge and James Walsh, Pontifi-
cal Institute of Medieval Studies, Toronto, 1978. (The
Introduction and Notes to this edition are of dubious
quality.)

*Julian of Norwich: A Revelation of Love*, Sloane 2499 MS, ed.
Marion Glasscoe, University of Exeter, 1993 (Rev. edn). (By
far the best edition.)

## Translations

*Julian of Norwich: Showings*, trans. Edmund Colledge and James
Walsh, CWS, New York, Paulist Press, 1978.

*Revelations of Divine Love*, trans. M. L. del Mastro, New York,
Doubleday, 1977.

*A Lesson of Love*, trans. Fr John-Julian, London, Darton, Longman & Todd, 1988.

*Revelations of Divine Love*, trans. Clifton Wolters, Harmondsworth, Penguin, 1966.

## PARAMYSTICAL WRITINGS

*Texts*

*Ancrene Wisse*, ed. J. R. R. Tolkien, EETS (OS 249), Oxford
University Press, 1962.

*The Mirror of St Edmund*, ed. C. Horstman, *Yorkshire Writers:
Richard Rolle of Hampole and his Followers*, London, Son-
nenschein, 1895, pp. 219–61.

*The Fire of Love*, ed. Ralph Harvey, EETS (OS 106), Oxford
University Press, 1896 (reprinted 1996).

*English Writings of Richard Rolle*, ed. Hope Emily Allen, Oxford
University Press, 1931.

*Richard Rolle: Prose and Verse*, ed. S. J. Ogilvie-Thomson, EETS (OS 293), Oxford University Press, 1988.

*The Book of Margery Kempe*, ed. Sanford B. Meech and Hope Emily Allen, EETS (OS 212), Oxford University Press, 1940.

*Translations*

*Ancrene Riwle*, trans. M. B. Salu, University of Exeter Press, 1990.

*Anchoritic Spirituality: Ancrene Wisse and Associated Works*, trans. Anne Savage and Nicholas Watson, *CWS*, New York, Paulist Press, 1991.

*The Fire of Love*, trans. Clifton Wolters, Harmondsworth, Penguin, 1972.

*The Book of Margery Kempe*, trans. B. A. Windeatt, Harmondsworth, Penguin, 1985.

## THEOLOGICAL BACKGROUND

Augustine, *The Essential Augustine*, ed. Vincent J. Bourke, Indianapolis, Hackett, 1974.

Augustine, *Augustine's Later Works*, trans. J. Burnaby, London, SCM Press, 1955.

Augustine, *Selected Writings*, trans. Mary T. Clark, *CWS*, New York, Paulist Press, 1984.

Augustine, *The Confessions*, trans. Henry Chadwick, Oxford University Press, 1991.

Augustine, *The Trinity*, trans. Edmund Hill, New York, New City Press, 1991.

Bernard of Clairvaux, *Sermons on the Song of Songs*, trans.

Killian Walsh and Irene Edmonds, Kalamazoo, Cistercian Fathers Series 4, 7, 31, 40, 1971–80.

Bernard of Clairvaux, *Selected Works*, trans. G. R. Evans, *CWS*, New York, Paulist Press, 1987.

Cassian, *Conferences*, trans. Colm Luibheid, *CWS*, New York, Paulist Press, 1985.

Guigo II, *The Ladder of Monks*, trans. Edmund Colledge and James Walsh, Oxford, Mowbray, 1978.

Hugh of St Victor, *Selected Spiritual Writings*, trans. A Religious of CSMV, London, Faber, 1962.

Pseudo-Dionysius, *The Complete Works*, trans. Colm Luibheid and Paul Rorem, *CWS*, New York, Paulist Press, 1987.

Richard of St Victor, *Selected Writings on Contemplation*, trans. Clare Kirchberger, London, Faber, 1957.

Richard of St Victor, *The Twelve Patriarchs, The Mystical Ark, Book Three of The Trinity*, trans. Grover A. Zinn, *CWS*, New York, Paulist Press, 1979.

William of St Thierry, *The Golden Epistle*, trans. Theodore Berkley, Kalamazoo, Cistercian Fathers Series 12, 1980.

## SECONDARY WORKS

Allchin, A. M., 'Julian of Norwich for Today', *Julian of Norwich: Four Studies*, Oxford, SLG Press, 1973.

Allchin, A. M., 'Julian and the Continuity of Tradition', *Julian: Woman of our Day*, ed. Robert Llewelyn, London, Darton, Longman & Todd, pp. 27–40.

Allchin, A. M., 'Julian of Norwich and Hildegard of Bingen', *Mount Carmel*, Vol. 37, No. 3, 1989, pp. 128–43.

Baker, Denise Nowakowski, *Julian of Norwich's Showings*, Princeton University Press, 1994.

Bauerschmidt, F. C., 'Julian of Norwich – Incorporated', *Modern Theology*, 13.1, January 1997, pp. 75–100.

Beckwith, Sarah, *Christ's Body: Identity, Culture and Society in Late Medieval Writings*, London, Routledge, 1993.

Beer, Frances, *Women and Mystical Experience in the Middle Ages*, Woodbridge, Boydell Press, 1992.

Bhattacharji, Santha, *God is an Earthquake*, London, Darton, Longman & Todd, 1997.

Bradley, Ritamary, *Julian's Way*, London, HarperCollins, 1992.

Bradley, Ritamary, *Not For The Wise*, London, Darton, Longman & Todd, 1994.

Bradley, Ritamary, 'The Speculum Image in Medieval Mystical Writers', *MMTE* III, 1984, pp. 9–27.

Bradley, Ritamary, 'Julian on Prayer', *Julian: Woman of our Day*, ed. Robert Llewelyn, London, Darton, Longman & Todd, 1985, pp. 61–74.

Bradley, Ritamary, 'The Goodness of God: A Julian Study', *Langland, The Mystics, and the Medieval Religious Tradition*, ed. Helen Phillips, Cambridge, D. S. Brewer, 1990, pp. 85–95.

Clark, J. P. H., 'The "Lightsome Darkness" – Aspects of Walter Hilton's Theological Background', *Downside Review* 95, 1977, pp. 95–109.

Clark, J. P. H., 'Walter Hilton and "Liberty of Spirit"', *Downside Review* 96, 1978, pp. 61–78.

Clark, J. P. H., 'The "Cloud of Unknowing", Walter Hilton and St John of the Cross: A Comparison', *Downside Review* 96, 1978, pp. 281–98.

Clark, J. P. H., 'Image and Likeness in Walter Hilton', *Downside Review* 97, 1979, pp. 204–20.

Clark, J. P. H., 'Action and Contemplation in Walter Hilton', *Downside Review* 97, 1979, pp. 258–74.

Clark, J. P. H., 'Sources and Theology in "The Cloud of Unknowing" ', *Downside Review* 98, 1980, pp. 83–109.

Clark, J. P. H., 'Nature, Grace and the Trinity in Julian of Norwich', *Downside Review* 100, 1982, pp. 203–20.

Clark, J. P. H., 'Walter Hilton in Defence of the Religious Life and the Veneration of Images', *Downside Review* 103, 1985, pp. 1–25.

Clark, J. P. H., 'The Trinitarian Theology of Walter Hilton's *Scale of Perfection* Book Two', *Langland, The Mystics, and the Medieval Religious Tradition*, ed. Helen Phillips, Cambridge, D. S. Brewer, 1990, pp. 125–40.

Clark, J. P. H., 'Time and Eternity in Julian of Norwich', *Downside Review* 109, 1991, pp. 259–76.

Clark, J. P. H., 'Late Fourteenth-Century Cambridge Theology and the English Contemplative Tradition', *MMTE* V, 1992, pp. 1–16.

Coakley, Sarah, 'Visions of the Self in Late Medieval Christianity: Some Cross-Disciplinary Reflections', *Philosophy, Religion, and the Spiritual Life*, ed. Michael McGhee, Cambridge University Press, 1992, pp. 89–103.

Davies, Oliver, *God Within: The Mystical Tradition of Northern Europe*, London, Darton, Longman & Todd, 1988.

Davies, Oliver, 'Transformational Processes in the Work of Julian of Norwich and Mechthild of Magdeburg', *MMTE* V, 1992, pp. 39–52.

Ellis, Roger, 'A Literary Approach to the Middle English Mystics', *MMTE* I, 1980, pp. 99–119.

Ellis, Roger, 'Margery Kempe's Scribe and the Miraculous

Books', *Langland, The Mystics, and the Medieval Religious Tradition*, ed. Helen Phillips, Cambridge, D. S. Brewer, 1990, pp. 161–75.

Ellis, Roger, 'Author(s), Compilers, Scribes and Biblical Texts: Did the *Cloud* Author translate the *Twelve Patriarchs*?', *MMTE* V, 1992, pp. 193–221.

Gatta, Julia, *A Pastoral Art: Spiritual Guidance in the English Mystics*, London, Darton, Longman & Todd, 1986.

Gillespie, Vincent, 'Mystic's Foot: Rolle and Affectivity', *MMTE* II, 1982, pp. 199–230.

Gillespie, Vincent, 'Strange Images of Death: The Passion in Later Medieval Devotional and Mystical Writing', *Analecta Cartusiana* 117, Band 3, 1987, pp. 110–59.

Gillespie, Vincent, 'Vernacular Books of Religion', *Book Production and Publishing in Britain 1375–1475*, ed. Jeremy Griffiths and Derek Pearsall, Cambridge University Press, 1989, pp. 317–44.

Gillespie, Vincent, 'Idols and Images: Pastoral Adaptations of *The Scale of Perfection*', *Langland, The Mystics, and the Medieval Religious Tradition*, ed. Helen Phillips, Cambridge, D. S. Brewer, 1990, pp. 97–123.

Gillespie, Vincent, 'Postcards from the Edge: Interpreting the Ineffable in the Middle English Mystics', *Interpretation: Medieval and Modern*, ed. Piero Boitani and Anna Torti, Cambridge, D. S. Brewer, 1993.

Gillespie, Vincent and Ross, Maggie, 'The Apophatic Image: The Poetics of Effacement in Julian of Norwich', *MMTE* V, 1992, pp. 53–77.

Gilson, Étienne, *The Mystical Theology of St Bernard*, Kalamazoo, Cistercian Publications, 1990.

Glasscoe, Marion, (ed.) *The Medieval Mystical Tradition in*

*England*, Vols I-V, Exeter Medieval English Texts and Studies, University of Exeter, 1980 and 1982; Cambridge, D. S. Brewer, 1984, 1987, and 1992.

Glasscoe, Marion, *English Medieval Mystics*, Longman, London, 1993.

Glasscoe, Marion, 'Means of Showing: An Approach to Reading Julian of Norwich', *Analecta Cartusiana* 106, 1983, pp. 155–77.

Glasscoe, Marion, 'Visions and Revisions: A Further Look at the Manuscripts of Julian of Norwich', *Studies in Bibliography*, Vol. 42, 1989, pp. 103–20.

Glasscoe, Marion, 'Time of Passion: Latent Relationships between Liturgy and Meditation in two Middle English Mystics', *Langland, The Mystics, and the Medieval Religious Tradition*, ed. Helen Phillips, Cambridge, D. S. Brewer, 1990, pp. 141–60.

Hamilton, Bernard, *Religion in the Medieval West*, London, Edward Arnold, 1986.

Hirsh, John C., *The Revelations of Margery Kempe*, Leiden, E. J. Brill, 1989.

Hussey, S. S., 'Walter Hilton: Traditionalist?', *MMTE* I, 1980, pp. 1–16.

Hussey, S. S., 'Editing the Middle English Mystics', *Analecta Cartusiana* 35, Band 2, 1983, pp. 160–73.

Jantzen, Grace, *Julian of Norwich*, London, SPCK, 1987.

Jones, Cheslyn, Wainwright, Geoffrey and Yarnold, Edward, (eds) *The Study of Spirituality*, London, SPCK, 1986.

Knowles, David, *The Religious Orders in England*, Vols 1–3, Cambridge University Press, 1948–59.

Knowles, David, *The English Mystical Tradition*, London, Burns and Oates, 1961.

Knowles, David, *The Evolution of Medieval Thought*, London, Longman, (2nd edn) 1988.

Leclercq, Jean, *The Influence of Saint Bernard*, Oxford, SLG Press, 1976.

Lees, Rosemary Ann, *The Negative Language of the Dionysian School of Mystical Theology*, 2 vols, *Analecta Cartusiana* 107, 1983.

Llewelyn, Robert, (ed.) *Julian: Woman of our Day*, London, Darton, Longman & Todd, 1985.

Llewelyn, Robert, *With Pity Not With Blame*, London, Darton, Longman & Todd, 1982.

Louth, Andrew, *Denys the Areopagite*, London, Geoffrey Chapman, 1989.

McGhee, Michael, (ed.) *Philosophy, Religion, and the Spiritual Life*, Cambridge University Press, 1992.

McGinn, Bernard, *The Foundations of Mysticism*, London, SCM Press, 1992.

McGinn, Bernard, *The Growth of Mysticism*, London, SCM Press, 1995.

McGinn, Bernard, 'Love, Knowledge, and Mystical Union in Western Christianity: Twelfth to Sixteenth Centuries', *Church History* 56, 1987, pp. 7–24.

*MMTE = The Medieval Mystical Tradition in England*, Vols I–V, ed. Marion Glasscoe, University of Exeter, 1980 and 1982; Cambridge, D. S. Brewer, 1984, 1987, and 1992.

Nuth, Joan M., *Wisdom's Daughter: The Theology of Julian of Norwich*, New York, Crossroad, 1991.

Pantin, W. A., *The English Church in the Fourteenth Century*, Cambridge University Press, 1955.

Park, Tarjei, 'Reflecting Christ: The Role of the Flesh in Walter Hilton and Julian of Norwich', *MMTE* V, 1992, pp. 17–37.

Pelphrey, Brant, *Love Was His Meaning: The Theology and Mysticism of Julian of Norwich*, Elizabethan and Renaissance Studies 92:4, Universität Salzburg, 1982.

Pelphrey, Brant, *Christ Our Mother*, London, Darton, Longman & Todd, 1989.

Phillips, Helen, (ed.) *Langland, The Mystics, and the Medieval Religious Tradition*, Cambridge, D. S. Brewer, 1990.

Raitt, Jill, with Bernard McGinn, John Meyendorff, Jean Leclercq, Louis Dupré, and Don E. Saliers, (eds) *Christian Spirituality*, Vols 1–3, London, SCM Press, 1989–90.

Riehle, Wolfgang, *The Middle English Mystics*, London, Routledge, 1981.

Sargent, Michael G., 'The Organization of *The Scale of Perfection*', *MMTE* II, 1982, pp. 231–61.

Sikka, Sonya, 'Transcendence in Death: A Heideggarian Approach to *Via Negativa* in *The Cloud of Unknowing*', *MMTE* V, 1992, pp. 179–92.

Swanson, John, 'Guide for the Inexpert Mystic', *Julian: Woman of our Day*, ed. Robert Llewelyn, London, Darton, Longman & Todd, 1985, pp. 75–88.

Swanson, R. N., *Religion and Devotion in Europe, c.1215–c.1515*, Cambridge University Press, 1995.

Thouless, Robert H., *The Lady Julian: A Psychological Study*, London, SPCK, 1924.

Tixier, René, ' "Good Gamesumli Pley", Games of Love in *The Cloud of Unknowing*', *Downside Review* 109, 1990, pp. 235–53.

Tugwell, Simon, *Ways of Imperfection*, London, Darton, Longman & Todd, 1984.

Underhill, Evelyn, *Mysticism*, London, Methuen, 1911.

Underhill, Evelyn, *The Mystics of the Church*, London, James Clarke & Co., 1925.

Upjohn, Sheila, *In Search of Julian of Norwich*, London, Darton, Longman & Todd, 1989.

Upjohn, Sheila, *Why Julian Now?*, London, Darton, Longman & Todd, 1997.

Wakefield, Gordon S., (ed.) *A Dictionary of Christian Spirituality*, London, SCM Press, 1983.

Ward, Benedicta, 'Lady Julian of Norwich and her Audience: "Mine Even-Christian"', *The English Religious Tradition and the Genius of Anglicanism*, ed. Geoffrey Rowell, Wantage, Ikon, 1992.

Ward, Benedicta and Leech, Kenneth, *Julian Reconsidered*, Oxford, SLG Press, 1988.

Watson, Nicholas, *Richard Rolle and the Invention of Authority*, Cambridge University Press, 1991.

Watson, Nicholas, 'The Trinitarian Hermeneutic in Julian of Norwich's *Revelation of Love*', *MMTE* V, 1992, pp. 79–100.

Watson, Nicholas, 'The Composition of Julian of Norwich's *Revelation of Love*', *Speculum* 68, 1993, pp. 637–83.

Williams, Rowan, *The Wound of Knowledge*, London, Darton, Longman & Todd, (Rev. edn) 1990.

Williams, Rowan, '"Know Thyself": What Kind of Injunction?', *Philosophy, Religion, and the Spiritual Life*, ed. Michael McGhee, Cambridge University Press, 1992, pp. 211–27.

Woods, Richard, (ed.) *Understanding Mysticism*, London, Athlone Press, 1980.

# Organizations

Contemplative prayer, like all prayer, is not an exercise in individualism. When we truly pray we are caught up into the life of God as the communion of saints where we experience our *relatedness* in Christ. If we are to grow in our prayer life, especially in the way of contemplative prayer, we need the personal encouragement, teaching and challenge of other Christians. To find a spiritual director you should visit your parish priest, and even if your priest feels unable personally to help you in the way of contemplation, they will know someone who can. For more general teaching and support the following organizations are particularly helpful. The first and last of these are the historical sites of the English Mystics to which the contemplative of today might make pilgrimage.

The Julian Centre and Shrine, St Julian's Alley, Rouen Road, Norwich, NR1 1QT. St Julian's Church (Anglican) contains the reconstructed cell of Julian. The Centre has a good library and friendly staff. It also has a good mail order list of publications relating to the English mystics and contemplative prayer.

The Julian Meetings, c/o Gail Ballinger, The Parsonage, Sambourne Lane, Sambourne, Redditch, B96 6PA. This is the source for information on the 'Julian Meetings', local ecumenical silent prayer groups.

*Mystics Quarterly*, Dept of English, University of Waikato, Private Bag 3105, Hamilton, New Zealand. Originally *The English Mystics Newsletter*, this journal contains lively academic work on medieval mystical texts.

The Order of Julian of Norwich (OJN), S10 W26392 Summit Avenue, Waukesha, Wisconsin 53188, USA. This Episcopalian order follows the traditional contemplative life and publishes good quality exposition of the English Mystics. It also supplies by mail order a good range of publications on contemplative prayer.

SLG Press, Convent of the Incarnation, Fairacres, Oxford, OX4 1TB. The Sisters of the Love of God, an enclosed, contemplative Anglican order, publish a variety of well-written contemplative studies and texts. A list of their publications will be sent to you if you write to them. Their journal, *Fairacres Chronicle*, contains illuminating essays on spirituality.

Walter Hilton's home, Thurgarton Priory, exists in the form of St Peter's

Church (Anglican), Thurgarton, Nottinghamshire. The church is a peaceful place, and contains the altar used in Hilton's day (and used by the current Vicar of Thurgarton!).

The Society for Promoting Christian Knowledge (SPCK) was
founded in 1698. It has as its purpose three main tasks:

- **Communicating the Christian faith in its rich diversity**

- **Helping people to understand the Christian faith
  and to develop their personal faith**

- **Equipping Christians for mission and ministry**

SPCK Worldwide serves the Church through Christian
literature and communication projects in over 100 countries.
Special schemes also provide books for those training for
ministry in many parts of the developing world. SPCK
Worldwide's ministry involves Churches of many traditions.
This worldwide service depends upon the generosity of others
and all gifts are spent wholly on ministry programmes,
without deductions.

SPCK Bookshops support the life of the Christian community
by making available a full range of Christian literature and other
resources, and by providing support to bookstalls and book agents
throughout the UK. SPCK Bookshops' mail order department
meets the needs of overseas customers and those unable to have
access to local bookshops.

SPCK Publishing produces Christian books and resources,
covering a wide range of inspirational, pastoral, practical and
academic subjects. Authors are drawn from many different
Christian traditions, and publications aim to meet the needs of a
wide variety of readers in the UK and throughout the world.

The Society does not necessarily endorse the individual views
contained in its publications, but hopes they stimulate readers to
think about and further develop their Christian faith.

For further information about the Society, please write to:
SPCK, Holy Trinity Church, Marylebone Road,
London NW1 4DU, United Kingdom.
Telephone: 0171 387 5282